Smith, Thomas

The Handbook of Iron Shipbuilding

Smith, Thomas

The Handbook of Iron Shipbuilding

ISBN/EAN: 9783867416757

First published in 2011 by Europaeischer Hochschulverlag GmbH & Co KG, Bremen, Germany.

© Europaeischer Hochschulverlag GmbH & Co KG, Fahrenheitstr. 1, D-28359 Bremen (www.ehv-online.com). All rights reserved.

This book is a reproduction of an out of print title and has originally been published in 1869. Because no electronic master copies of this title could be obtained, the publisher had to reuse old copies of the text. We therefore apologize for any possible loss in quality.

EHV

THE HANDBOOK

OF

IRON SHIPBUILDING.

By THOMAS SMITH, M.I.N.A.
LONDON AND DUBLIN.

LONDON:
E. & F. N. SPON, 48, CHARING CROSS.
1869.

PREFACE.

The author being aware of the generally expressed want in all books published on the subject of Iron Shipbuilding—in many of which the theory of the lines, displacement, &c., are treated as if for the especial benefit of a Senior Wrangler at Cambridge, and utterly useless to the Shipbuilder and others, as the *practical part* is either very slightly touched upon, or entirely ignored—wishes to supply this void, without entering into theoretical investigations, which when written are seldom or never read. He has, during a long and varied experience, extending over twenty years in different parts of the United Kingdom, been at great pains to include in his notes such information as is really useful, carefully eliminating what has been, during the rapid advance of the science of Shipbuilding, shown to be superfluous or obsolete.

He has constantly kept in view two objects:—

Firstly. To make this a useful handbook for the Shipowner, not only regarding the construction of a vessel, but also as to the cost of work in all the great centres of the shipbuilding trade in the United Kingdom.

Secondly. He has been careful to study the requirements of the Shipbuilder, and it will be found particularly useful in making estimates, not only regarding the principal parts of the work, but also as a reminder of the various odds and ends which are frequently overlooked. And as a guide as to what the author, judging from his experience, deems the *quickest*, *cheapest*, and *best* system of doing the work.

Having the greatest respect for the dearly-bought experience, which is the result of years of actual toil, he considers that literature has the important part to perform of registering, arranging, and disseminating the experience of individuals. He therefore hopes that this, his contribution as a Naval Architect and Shipbuilder, will be accepted by those for whose use it is intended, *viz.* Shipowners, Shipbuilders, Inspectors, Ship Masters, Foremen, and intelligent working men, entirely as a practical guide, without any embellishment or attempt at elegance of composition, and only containing *plain facts, plainly stated*.

The Author is aware that it is the idea of many persons connected with the Shipbuilding TRADE to keep all matters relating to cost and detail of construction as secret as possible; but he looks upon publicity as one of the essentials of the present age, and those who DARE NOT explain the rules on which they work, with the full confidence of still being able to maintain their standing in their PROFESSION, are not made of the stuff that will win in these days; and secrecy is really too scarce for there to be any occasion to regard it as of any considerable value.

INTRODUCTION.

It is of the utmost importance that the reader of the following chapters on the various operations in the construction of Iron Ships should bear in mind that there is a regular order of succession to be adhered to; also that the omission of any one, or the interference with their order will be productive of much trouble, expense, and annoyance, just as the result as a whole will depend upon the careful and conscientious observation of the rules laid down in detail. We would, therefore, earnestly urge upon the reader's attention the necessity of keeping the foregoing observations in mind, as if actually appended to the head of each paragraph, since *bad work*, caused by *carelessness* or *ignorance*, is not only injurious to the public welfare and the reputation of the builder, but also disgraceful to the age in which we live.

CONTENTS.

	PAGE
Practical Iron Shipbuilding	1
Keels	1
Flat Plate Keels	3
Stern Posts and Stern Frames	3
Stems	4
Rudder Frames	4
Rudder Bands	5
Rudder Stops	5
Angle Iron Frames	6
Reverse Frames	8
Angle Irons on Beams	9
Floor Plates	11
Main-Deck Stringers	11
'Tween-Deck Stringers	12
Poop-Deck Stringers	12
Wash Plates	13
Bilge Keelsons, &c.	14
Bulkheads	15
Inside Sheerstrakes	17
Outside Sheerstrakes	18
Beams	18
Poop Beams	18
Framing of Hatches	19
Outside Plating	21
Weights per Foot of various sized Plate and Bulb-iron Beams, with Two-angle Irons and Rivets	25
Weights per Yard of Rivets	25
Weights of Deck Screws, Deck Bolts, Nails, Rooves, Dumps, Copper Bolts, &c.	26
Result of Experiment with three Pieces of Ship's Beams	27
Strength and Weight of Flax Canvas	28
Weights of Rivets of various Sizes	28
Average Allowance for Waste on converting Timber for Shipbuilding Purposes	29
Cost of Paints per Gallon, and the Superficial Area they will cover	29
Weight of Lineal Feet of Angle Iron, Equal Sided	30
Weights of Chain Cables	30
Number of Cubic Feet allowed in Chain Lockers for various sized Cables	31
Weights of one Cubic Foot of Timber, from actual Experiment	31
Formulæ for approximating the Gross Register Tonnage	31
Formulæ for approximating the Weight of Outside Plating for Iron Sailing-vessels	32

	PAGE
Rates of Wages per Day of the various Trades employed in Iron Shipbuilding	32
Thames District	32
Mersey	32
Tyne, Wear, and Tees	33
Clyde	33
Shipwrights' Work (Cost of)	34
East Coast of England	34
Iron Sailing-ship, 1440 Tons	34
Screw Steamer, 943 Tons	35
Launching a Ship of 1000 Tons	36
Thames District	36
Paddle Steamer, 687 Tons	36
Screw Steamer, 1023 Tons	37
Clyde District	37
Screw Steamer, 1063 Tons	37
Paddle Steamer, 1557 Tons	38
Allowance made by Shipwrights for Apprentices, when employed on Contract Work	38
Caulkers' Work (Thames)	39
Boat Building	39
Cost of five Pine Boats	39
Cost of one Larch Boat	41
Cost of Diagonal-built Boats	41
Prices for Iron Work paid in the generality of the Thames Building Yards	41
Prices for Iron Work in some of the Thames Yards, differing in some points from the above	46
Cost of Iron Work in the Yards on the East Coast of England	47
Sailing Ship of 500 Tons	47
Screw Steamer of 500 Tons	49
Screw Steamer of 800 Tons	50
Sailing Ship of 800 Tons	50
Iron Decks	51
Average Cost of Wages per Ton Weight of Material	50
Cost of Vessels built on the East Coast of England	51
Paddle Steamer, 665 Tons	51
Sailing Ship, 755 Tons	53
Screw Steamer, 315 Tons	54
Sailing Ship, 555 Tons	54
Cost of Vessels built on the Clyde District	56
Screw Steamer, 699 Tons	56
Screw Steamer, 722 Tons	57
Iron Work	57
Sundries	58
Wood Work	59
Outfit	60
Epitome	61
Working Expenses	61

PRACTICAL IRON SHIPBUILDING.

Keels.—In boring keel-bars, be particular to have the top row of rivet-holes marked no lower down than is necessary to make a good and close fit of the garboard strake at the top row of holes; and on no account weaken the keel bar by having the lower row of holes bored too low down; at the same time, care must be taken to have a distance equal to the diameter of rivets between the lower edge of upper row and upper edge of bottom row; *i.e.* a distance of two diameters between the centre lines of the top and bottom rows. In marking off the holes, attention should be paid to having them properly divided; that is to say, having the upper rivet exactly between the two lower rivets.

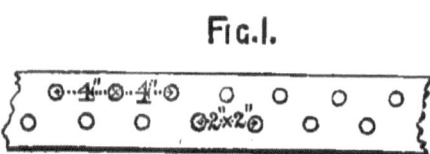

Fig. I.

Make the length of scarfs of keel-bars at least ten times the thickness of keel-bar. Lloyd's Rules give only eight times, but this is too little to make a substantial connection.

Before commencing to drill the scarfs, have them drawn perfectly close, and see that the ends are brought together, and are a good fit.

It is not necessary to drill more than three holes in scarfs for *stitching*, and these should be on top part, so as not to weaken the keel-bar more than necessary.

The upper side of scarf should be caulked before the frames are laid across keel and the under side after the keel-plates are riveted.

The butts of the garboard strake must be spaced so as to be well clear of the butts of keel-bar; say at least 30 inches, when practicable, and with care this distance can generally be given.

Have the position of all frames marked on the keel with a centre punch before any of the frames are laid across; this will save a deal of unnecessary trouble.

See that the keel-bars are properly shored, straightened on top edge, and got quite fair previous to laying any frames over them. Attention must also be paid to fairing the keel fore and aft by a line, after the frames are up in place, before commencing to fit any of the garboard strake on.

It is important to keep the keel a reasonable height from the ground, so as to allow room for the workmen to get under the vessel's bottom without being too much confined; otherwise they cannot make good work of the riveting and caulking. In

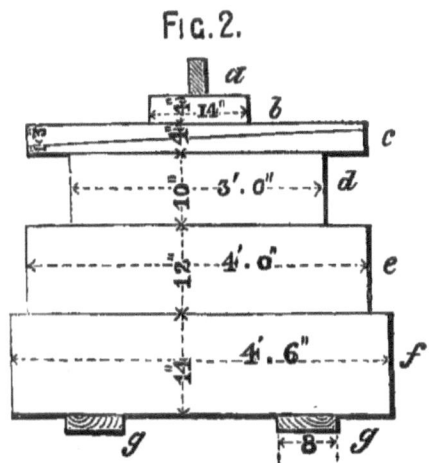

a. Keel.   *b.* Cap Piece of Oak.   *c.* Gluts or Wedges.   *d.* Redpine.
e. Redpine.   *f.* Redpine.   *g.* Slabs.

settling this point you must bear in mind—if the vessel has a flat floor the blocks must be laid higher.

Let the keel-blocks be spaced about 7 feet 6 inches apart, and have a double block between, say every second and third block, alternately. This will allow for shifting any blocks that may be necessary to get at the work without fear of the vessel settling down. Have the three or four last blocks laid on fore and aft logs, as the vessel will be certain to sink at after end, if anywhere.

Fig. 2 shows height and dimension for keel-blocks, suitable for vessels of the usual run.

It is well to have the keel riveted as soon as possible to prevent dirt or any rubbish getting down between the keel and garboard strake.

Flat-Plate Keels.—If for a vessel building to class at Lloyd's, the breadth and thickness must be as follows:—In vessels of 500 tons and under, 2 feet wide; from 500 to 1000 tons, 2 feet 6 inches wide; 1000 tons and upwards, 3 feet wide. The thickness of plates in all cases to be not less than one and a half times the thickness of the garboard strake. The foregoing rule gives a good scantling for such keels, and I would recommend it to be adhered to in all cases.

It is desirable in flat-plate keels that the butts of the garboard strake should be clear of the butts of keel-plates at least two spaces of frames on both the port and starboard sides; and for this reason, the keel-plates should be made in such lengths as will suit this; also see that the butts of the keel-plates are fair between two frames, as this is necessary to facilitate the putting on of the butt-straps.

In all cases it is recommended to treble-rivet the butts of keel-plate, making the butt-straps as wide as can be got in between the flange of the frame angle-irons and heel-pieces on next frame.

Stern-Posts and Stern-Frames.—In a screw steamer, care must be taken in boring any holes about the boss that may be required, and this should be done previous to putting the frame up in place. Mark off the lead of these holes so that they may be bored in the proper direction, and thereby have a proper divide on the inside of the boss.

Particular attention should be paid to taking out any twist that may be in the stern-frame when it comes from the forge, and be careful to see that the bosses on both outer and inner post lead fair fore and aft.

In the upper portion of stern-posts it is only necessary to have one row of rivets for the rudder trunk. Some builders and inspectors prefer to put two rows, but it is only waste of time doing so.

In the riveting of bosses, it is absolutely necessary to have the countersink bored out a sufficient depth, so that when the engineers have done boring and fitting in the stern-tube, there will be plenty of countersink left to hold the rivets secure.

In putting in the boss-rivets it is a good plan to cool them at the points, so that the heads may thereby be well tightened up.

Bear in mind that it will save trouble and make better workmanship if you arrange the plating so that a strake will cover the boss.

Make the scarf of your stern-post always on the port side, and do not have the length of the knee or keel portion to exceed 10 feet 6 inches, as that length is about as great as can be conveniently taken on ordinary trucks, if the post has to come by railway from the forge.

Stems.—The mould for bending the stem too should be made off the inside line of stem, and if it is not turned before the scarfs of keel-bars are cut and finished, it is well to measure the total length of the keel on the blocks, and contract or increase the length of the stem-bar as the case may require to make up the exact length. Do not drill any holes in stem until it is turned to shape, and be careful to have the scarf on the right side to agree with forward length of keel-bar.

In forging stem-bars have the fore-side shaped to a flat half-round, and see that there is no twist in the bar.

Rudder-Frames.—Should you make the rudder forging in

scantling, according to Lloyd's, bear in mind that if for a spar-deck ship, or vessel with full poop and forecastle, the diameter of the rudder-head must be in accordance with the dimension given for the gross tonnage, and not the tonnage under main deck.

Attention should be paid to having the rudder-pintles all in a fair line. Have a steel washer for the pintle at heel of rudder to work on. It is always the best plan to make the rudder to unship, and the space for unshipping at each pintle should be about one inch deeper than the length of the pintle.

In a screw vessel attention should be paid to keeping the pintles clear of the bracket on the after-post for outside shaft bearing.

In rudder forging for vessels of from 200 to 500 tons, have a stay across centre of rudder from rudder-post to bow; and in vessels over that tonnage, two stays; width of stays about $3\frac{1}{2}$ inches. The stays may either be made with the forging or of cast-iron fitted in. The space between the plates of rudder should be filled in with either wood or Portland cement. Thickness of rudder-plates need in no case exceed $\frac{1}{4}$ inch; and it makes the most substantial work to have the rudder-plates snap riveted.

Rudder-bands.—Pay particular attention to see that the centre of pintles are correctly set off before boring same, by striking a line up centres, to see if these are in a line and that the back is straight and fair; this applies also to the sternpost. See that the rudder-trunk is made of sufficent size to allow the rudder-stock to be got up easily, say from 8 to 9 inches internal diameter for a 4 to 5 inch rudder-post; other diameters to be in like proportion. Attention should be paid to having the rudder-trunk and angle-iron binding the foot of trunk to outside plating a good fit, and the bottom carefully caulked.

Rudder-stops.—The proper angle for a rudder to travel is 42 degrees on each side of centre line of ship, and the stoppers should be made to suit this. Be particular to have the stops made strong enough and well secured to sternpost. The rudder working easily is a matter of great importance, and requires particular attention in the lining-off and putting in place.

Angle-iron Frames.—Previous to putting any work on the bars, have them examined to see that there are no cracks or blemishes, as angle-bars are constantly sent from the Ironworks without care being taken to see if they are sound.

In punching the frames, see that the holes are properly divided; and as an example, for double-riveted laps with $\frac{3}{4}$-inch rivets, have the top hole $4\frac{1}{2}$ inches from upper edge of lap, or $6\frac{1}{2}$ inches from centre of lap, and the lower hole $3\frac{3}{4}$ inches from lower edge of lap, or 6 inches from centre of lap, on plate mark

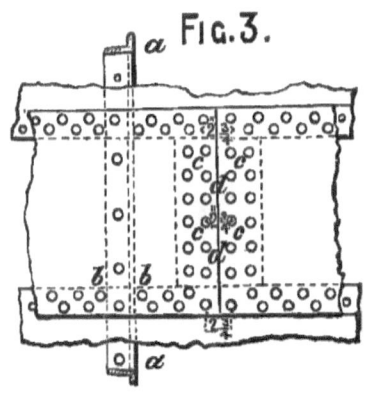

a. Frame.
b. Rivets to be as close to frame as head of rivet will permit.
c c c. Chain-riveting at butts to have the holes punched opposite each other.
d d. Butt-straps to be fitted as close as possible between laps of outside strakes.

on the mould on board. Fig. 3 shows the proper spacing of rivets for double-riveted laps with $\frac{3}{4}$-inch rivets.

In single laps have a hole punched $5\frac{1}{2}$ inches each side of centre of lap, the lap being $2\frac{3}{4}$ inches. Divide the spacing of holes for rivets between one lap of plates and the next, as near to eight times the diameter of the rivet as you possibly can arrange.

In frames that run up to form sides of poop, forecastle, or

bridge, have those with no beam on, cut off low enough to allow the lug-pieces for securing stringer-plate to shell to run from beam to beam. Fig. 4. A hole should be punched in head of

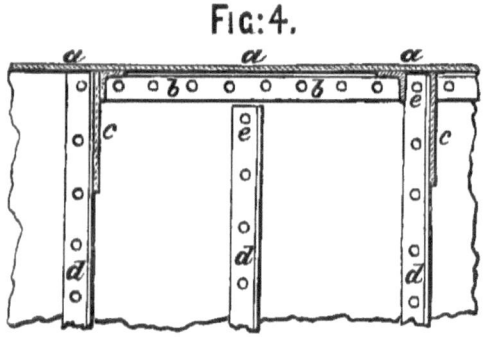

a a a. Poop-deck Stringer-plate.   *b b.* Lug.   *c c.* Beam-knees.
d d d. Frames.   *e e.* This hole to be made after the plating is on.

the frames that are cut short for lug-pieces passing, about 3 inches down; but it is best not to put this in until the vessel is framed and faired.

In frames that step on the knee of sternpost or stem, do not neglect to have them cut to the proper thickness to allow the plating to come on.

The heel of frames bearing on keel should be carefully cut and finished, so as to butt close together, and the bearance not to be greater in width than the thickness of keel, otherwise a proper job will not be made of the garboard strake.

The inside flange of angle-iron frame should be punched so as to suit size of the reverse frame, and care should be taken to see that the holes are so punched as to take the centre of flange of reverse frame.

It is necessary to see that the heel-pieces are quite fair with under-side of frames, and that they bear true on the keel. One or two holes only should be punched in the frames, for the beam-knee, prior to putting up the frames.

Length of beam-knee is measured square off, and the holes should be divided round the sweep, the centre of lower hole placed about 2 inches from lower edge of knee. Fig. 5.

Do not have the upper hole in head of frame for upper rivet in beam-knee punched until the frames of vessel are all faired

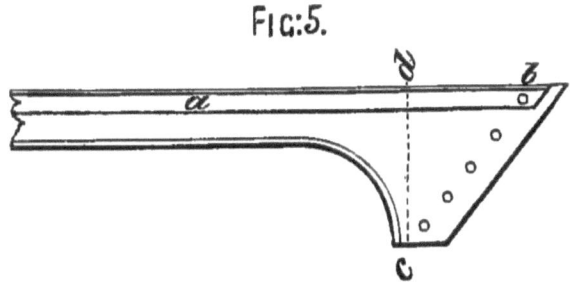

FIG: 5.

a. Reverse Iron.   *b.* This hole punched to take reverse bar on beam.
c d. This measurement at right angles to top of beam—not obliquely.

and sheered, as in case the beam requires to be lifted or lowered, it spoils the hole, and as this rivet passes through the angle-iron on beam it is necessary the hole should be true to make good work. The same rule applies to the bottom hole in beam-knee, as it looks very unworkmanlike to see a blind hole there.

The double frames at the bulkheads should be punched for rivets 4 inches centre to centre, and should be chipped at both edges previous to hoisting up in place, otherwise difficulty will be found in making a tight job of the caulking.

If the vessel has a sheerstrake with jump joints, see that the holes punched in frames are clear of the lap of both the inside and outside sheerstrake.

Reverse Frames.—The frames with no beams on to have the reverse bars running up to main-deck height, and these to butt in centre of floor, having heel-pieces of angle-iron on opposite side of floor top, of sufficient size to form top flange for keelson-fastenings.

Short reverse frames to run up to upper turn of bilge; but if there is a spirketting plate on 'tween-deck stringer, then the short reverse frames should run up to top of said plate.

Butts of the short reverse frames should be about 4 feet each side of centre-line, alternately on the starboard and port side;

but should these butts come in the way of boiler or other keelsons, the distance must be altered to suit.

Holes should not be punched in reverse frames in way of floor-ends, unless there is a clear space of three-quarters-of-an-

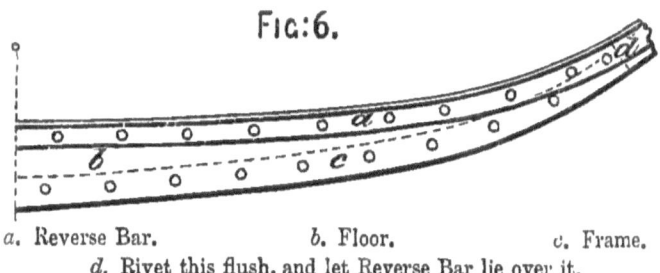

Fig: 6.

a. Reverse Bar.   *b.* Floor.   *c.* Frame.
d. Rivet this flush, and let Reverse Bar lie over it.

inch from outside of rivet-hole to lower edge of reverse frame. Fig. 6.

The reverse frames across the floor-tops at ends of vessel will require to be bevelled to suit the rise of floors and make a fair seat for the centre keelson. These bevels can best be taken when the vessel is ribanded and shored up.

See that the butts of the reverse frames are quite close and fair to each other. Accuracy of the workmanship adds greatly to the strength in all parts of an iron vessel.

The reverse frames must fit well over the floor-ends, and see that the floor-ends are thinned down to suit this.

The double reverse frame on floor-top should be neatly fitted on. Get a straight-edge, to see that it is fair, and attend to having all the scarphing or lug pieces riveted close to floor-plates.

Angle-irons on Beams.—The holes must be punched to suit width of deck-planks; the centre should be marked on the beam and have two template battens made for marking the holes for punching in the angle-irons, so that they are equally spaced and divided. The holes for the fore-and-aft tie-plates and stringer-plates should also be set off on these battens and the holes marked and punched accordingly. Holes for tie-plates and stringer must be punched to suit the diameter of rivets intended to be used, and those for the deck-plank to suit size of deck screws or bolts.

Holes should not be punched nearer to beam-ends on top flange of angle-iron on beam than about 6 or 7 inches, in case they should not come fair with the stringer angle-iron holes. These holes are best drilled through top flange of beam angle-iron, after the stringer is put on, the holes, of course, being previously punched in the stringer-plate.

One angle-iron only on beam to run out to beam-end, and

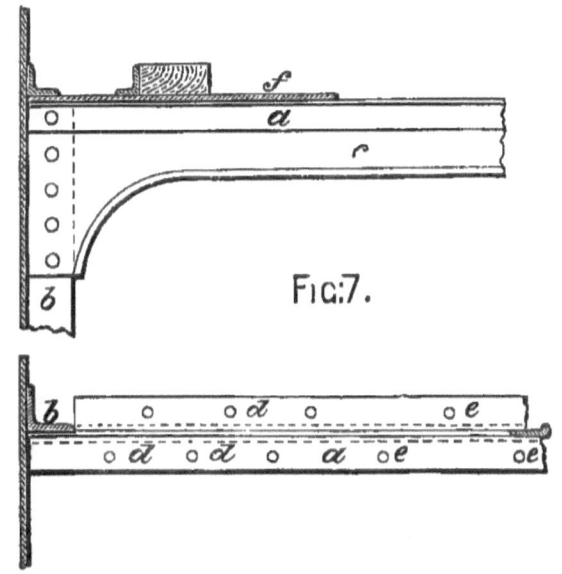

FIG. 7.

a. Reverse Bar on Beam.   *b b.* Frame.   *c.* Beam.
d d d. Rivets for Stringer-plate, 6″ or 7″ apart.
e e e. Ditto for Deck-plank twice the width of plank.   *f.* Stringer-plate.

to take a rivet through angle-iron on beam-knee and frame. Fig. 7.

The holes for riveting stringer-plate to angle-iron on beams should be about eight times the diameter of the rivets apart.

Attention should be paid to see that the angle-irons on beams are properly levelled at each end, so as to give a true seat on which to rivet the stringer-plates.

Floor-plates.—Floors should be twice the height above keel at floor-ends that they are at centre-line, and should be parallel to base-line athwartships, as far as practicable. Floor-plates at ends to be the width of inside flange of angle-iron frames.

See that the floor-ends are neatly thinned down, so that the reverse-frames fit over fair and close.

Floor-plates should be sheared half-an-inch less than the shape of frames.

The floor-ends where they have been thinned down for reverse frames should be chipped flush with the frame, both inside and out, previous to keelson or shell plating going on.

Limber-holes should be cut so as to clear frames, heel-pieces, lug-pieces for keelsons, intercostals, &c.

At the extreme ends of vessel, the floor-plates should be increased in depth to say twice the depth of floors amidships,

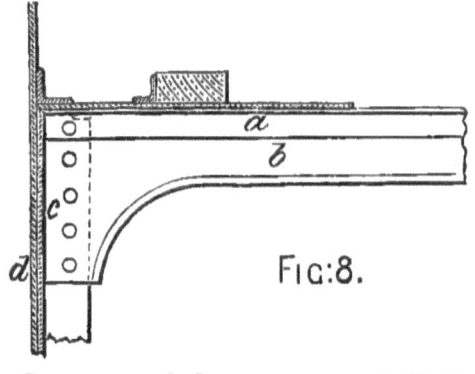

Fig: 8.

a. Reverse Bar.   b. Beam.   c. Inside Sheerstrake.
d. Outside Sheerstrake.

or until they measure say 2 feet across the top, from outside to outside of frame.

Floor-plate for the transom-frame should be put on the depth of the knuckle, so that the stern timbers are sufficiently secured.

Main-deck Stringer.—In the case of an inside sheerstrake going up only to underside of main-deck stringer-plate, the holes in said stringer for the angle-iron bar will require punching the thickness of the inside sheerstrake nearer the outer edge of stringer-plate, so as to catch the centre of the bar. Fig. 8.

Should the inside sheerstrake not run up above the main-deck stringer-plate, see that the stringer projects over the frames the full thickness of the inside sheerstrake.

Attention should be paid to punching the holes in stringer-plate for the angle-iron bar, to see that they are not punched with the same die as is used for the outside plating, no more countersink being required than is sufficient to keep the punch from choking, and the stringer-plates should be well sheared to form of side of vessel, or a bad bearing will be left for the gunwale angle-iron bars.

It is advisable to have the stringer-plates riveted to the beams, also the butt-straps riveted as soon as possible, and see that the butts come well clear of butts of sheerstrake.

Previous to commencing with main-deck stringer, see that the heads of frames and reverse frames are not higher than the beams.

Have all holes for the diagonal tie-plates in main-deck stringer-plates punched before putting in place. It is well in all cases to have the butts of main-deck stringers treble-chain riveted.

'Tween-deck Stringer.—Have all beams in and riveted before commencing to put in 'tween-deck stringers.

In vessels where the alternate reverse frames do not run up to height of hold-beams, see that holes are not punched in the vertical flange of stringer angle-iron, unless it is intended to rivet a lug-piece on the frame, for fastening the stringer angle-iron to the frames with no reverse bar running to that height.

In the after-peake, where there is a considerable flare in the sides of vessel, it is advisable to use a bar of larger dimensions for the stringer angle-iron, so as to get a good hole in the bar, not too near the edge, and thereby weaken it considerably. Fig. 9.

Poop-deck Stringer.—In putting on poop and forecastle deck stringers, have the stringer-plate sheared to come out to the outside edge of frames; so that when the forecastle or poop plating goes on it will butt up against it.

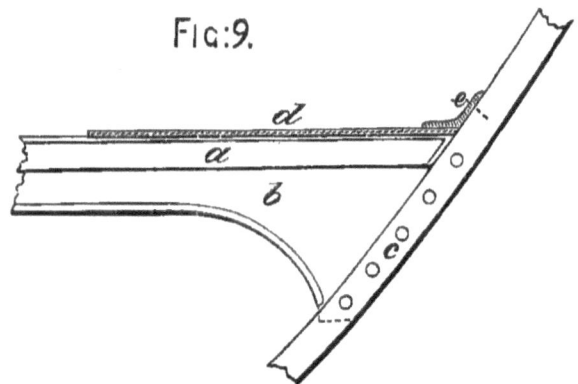

Fig: 9.

a. Reverse Bar.   *b.* Beam.   *c.* Frame.   *d.* Stringer-plate.
e. Rivet must not be too near edge of angle-iron, nor too far down in its bosom.

Holes should be punched in edge of centre stringer-plate aft, for fastening plate, for taking rudder-trunk, and fixing stuffing-box round rudder-head to.

Wash-plates.—Do not put wash-plates between bulkheads and floor-plate on adjoining frames, so as to allow the water to get freely to the pumps.

Fitting-in wash-plates between floors may be done as shown

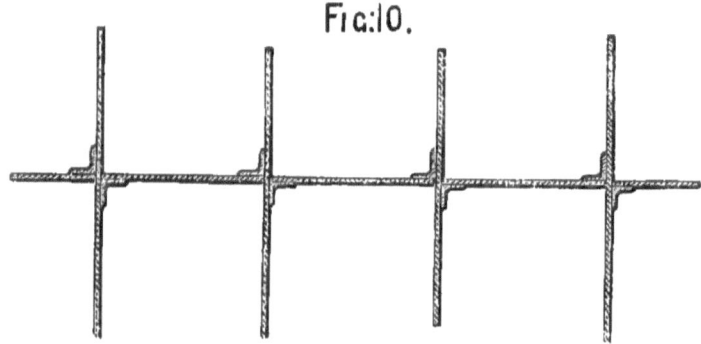

Fig:10.

in Fig. 10; but if they are required to serve as intercostal keelsons, four angle-irons at each floor will be necessary, and they must be made to fit close on.

Bilge-Keelsons, &c.—In putting on the lug-pieces for keelsons, see that they are quite fair with the edge of inside flange of angle-iron frame, and the fore-and-aft flange of reverse frame.

The lug-pieces should fit close against the frame angle-iron, and be well riveted thereto.

In keelsons formed of two angle-irons with a bulb-iron between allow between the angle-irons a quarter-of-an-inch extra, beyond the thickness of the bulb-iron, in marking off the holes for rivets in reverse frames and lug-pieces as far as the bulb-iron extends.

The lug-pieces for three frames forward and aft of the finish of bulb-iron between angles should not be punched, but drilled to suit a tapered slip neatly fitted between the two keelson angle-bars.

The butts of angle-iron bars of keelsons should be so shifted as to be at least two spaces of frames clear of butts of other keelsons, and as far as practicable clear of butts of outside plating.

If the angle-irons for keelsons are 4 inches or more, the

FIG. 11.

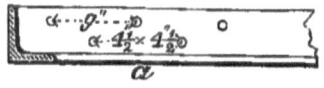

a. In some cases, 5″.

holes for rivets should be punched each side of the centre-line (Fig. 11).

Athwartship flanges of bilge-keelson angle-irons in way of breasthooks should not be riveted till the breasthook-plate is in.

See that the breasthooks are got in as soon as possible, and that they are well fitted and securely riveted in place. A manhole should be cut in breasthooks where necessary.

Should the breasthooks or pointers aft in a screw-vessel not be high enough above the stern-tube, they should not be riveted until the boss for shaft is bored and finished, on account of leaving room for men fastening bolts, &c.

Have the position of bilge-keelsons carefully marked off on frames, and see that they are sheered fair.

It is advisable to keep the bilge-keelsons clear of ribbons as far as possible, in case the lug-pieces or reverse frames want any setting up.

When practicable, have the height of lower bilge-keelsons at aft-peake bulkhead made to correspond with the height of top

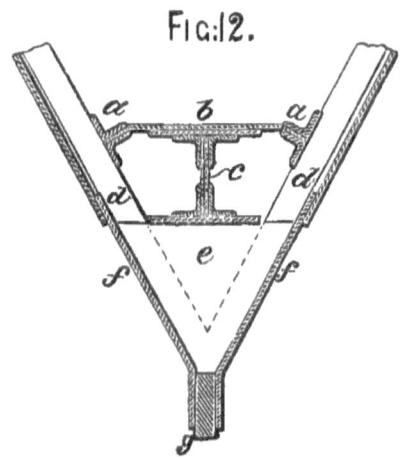

FIG. 12.

a a. Bilge-keelsons.   *b.* Breasthook.   *c.* Centre-keelson.   *d.* Frame.
     e. Floor.   *f.* Garboard Strake.   *g.* Keel.

plate of centre keelson, so as to get a breasthook plate riveted between the bilge-keelson angle-irons and top of centre keelson (Fig. 12). This makes a good finish and a very secure fastening.

Bulkheads.—See that the bulkhead-frames are all chipped fair on edges, prior to putting up in place, so that the bulkhead plates can be properly caulked under the shelf-plates, stringers, &c.

The bulkhead-plates should be caulked outside between the frames, as well as both sides inside, and round the edges of the gravit-plates, for keelsons passing through, see that the gravit-plates are a good fit and neatly put on. The plates for gravits should be one-eighth of an inch thicker than the bulkhead-plates.

The beam angle-bars should be cut short on bulkheads, so that they lie in the bosom of the bar (see Fig. 13), and the

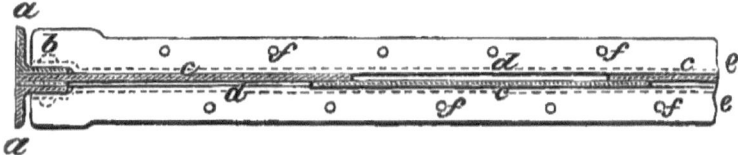

Fig. 13.

a. Side-frame.
b. These holes to be left blind, and riveted after the rest of bulkhead.
c c. Bulkhead Plates.
d d. Slip to be set to curve of beam, and to equal angle-iron in depth.
e e. The vertical flanges of these bars not to be less than 3′ to get a good rivet in head of vertical bar.
f f f Holes to suit deck-planks.

angle-irons forming the beam on bulkhead should be not less than 3 inches deep, so that a good rivet may be got in through the head of the vertical angle-iron bar. The vertical bars should have a hole for a rivet punched through both side-frames

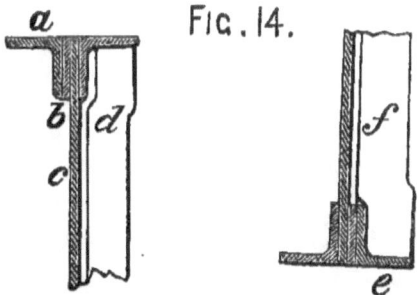

Fig. 14.

a. Beam's Reverse Bar. b. Slip. c. Bulkhead-plate.
d. Vertical Bar, to be properly joggled over. e. Side-frames.
f. Vertical Bar.

and should be neatly joggled for it at foot. The same applies to both the reverse angle-irons on the top edge (see Fig. 14).

In plating bulkheads, attention should be paid to see that the first plate is at right-angles with the keel; also see that the reverse angles forming the beam are not sagged down in centre or standing too high at centre or ends.

The fore and after peake bulkheads should be plated in the vessel, after the frames are faired, not from the mould, or board, in case the frames may not be the proper fit at the bottom. This applies more especially to vessels with flat-plate keels.

Attention should be paid to the fitting and punching of the gravit plates, to see that the holes are sufficiently close and regular, and that the plates are not made larger than necessary; as, if so, they cannot be caulked tight. It is also advisable to have a rivet as close as practicable to the hole for keelson-bars passing through the bulkhead (Fig 15).

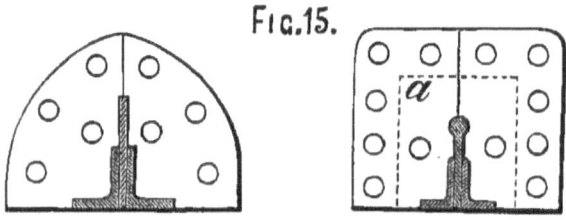

a. Boiler-keelsons in engine-room.

Inside Sheerstrakes.—The butts of inside sheerstrake should be double-riveted through inside sheerstrake and butt strap; the row of rivets next butt of plate to be riveted flush before the outside sheerstrake is put on (Fig. 16).

If there is only one frame between the butts of outside and inside sheerstrake, see that the plates are butted fair in the centre, between frames. Same rule applies to the outside sheerstrake, so that there is a full frame space of shift between the butts of outside and inside sheerstrakes.

The holes for rivets in the gunwale angle-iron bars should not be punched with the same die as used for outside plating, on account of giving too much countersink.

In inside or ordinary sheerstrakes attention should be paid

to seeing that the holes for the vertical flange of gunwale angle-iron are punched the proper height, so that the holes may be fair in the centre of bar.

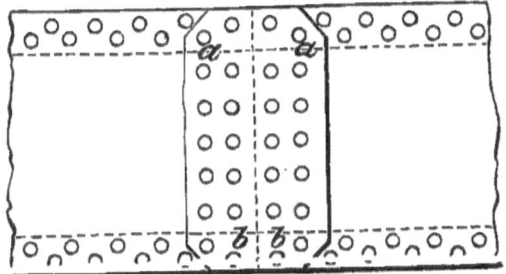

Fig. 16.

a a. These two rows, through inside and outside sheerstrakes and butt-strap, &c.
b b. These two rows through inside sheerstrake, and butt-straps, and riveted flush, before outside plate is put on.

Outside Sheerstrakes. — In outside sheerstrakes, make sure that the gunwale angle-iron bars on the top edge of sheerstrake are properly faired all fore and aft, as also the top edge of the sheerstrake itself. If possible, it is well that the gunwale angle-bar should be not less than 4 inches by 4 inches, as this width will give a better chance of making all fair holes.

Beams.—The beam-mould should be made the full breadth of the vessel, so that the total length of beam can be taken off and the correct bevel taken at both sides. The mould should be made the full depth of the beam-knees.

Have the bottom hole for rivet in the beam-knee punched, so as to allow an inch-and-a-half of iron from the under-side of rivet to bottom of knee.

Poop-Beams.—Have the poop-beams put up and bolted to the frames, but do not have them riveted until after the stringer plates and tie plates are all faired and riveted. This should be specially attended to, as it frequently occurs that if the beams are riveted first the knees get twisted, and set the beams up or down, as the case may be, making bad and unfair work of the stringer and tie plates.

To keep the poop-beams the proper spacing, it is a good plan to have a long plank, say in scantling, about 8 inches by 3 inches or 2½ inches, and have marked off on this plank the spacing of the beams, cutting out a notch for each beam; and when the beams are put up let them go into the notches, and have the plank shored up from main deck. By attending to this you will have all your beams equal distant and to one curve, which will add considerably to the appearance of the cabin ceiling, &c.

Framing of Hatches, &c.—In making hatches, put in the fore and aft angle-iron bars first; have them made a good and neat fit; see that they are straight fore and aft, and then put in the bulb iron or plate for fore-and-aft carlings; seeing this is also a good fit.

An angle-iron bar, about 5 inches by 5 inches by ½ inch, cut in lengths to suit, and fitted in the corners of the hatches, makes a much better finish than to knee the bulb-iron or bend the plate-knee.

The beams that form the fore-and-aft ends of hatchways should have reverse angle-irons, not less than 3 inches deep,

Fig. 17.

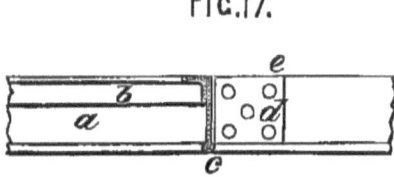

a. Beam.   *b.* Reverse Bar on beam.   *c.* Fore and after.
d. Plate-knee, in corner of hatch, inside.
e. This rivet to be not less than ¾ from edge.

so that the holes in plate-knees may be punched to allow three quarters of an inch of iron from top of rivet hole to top of knee-plate (Fig. 17).

Fig. 18.

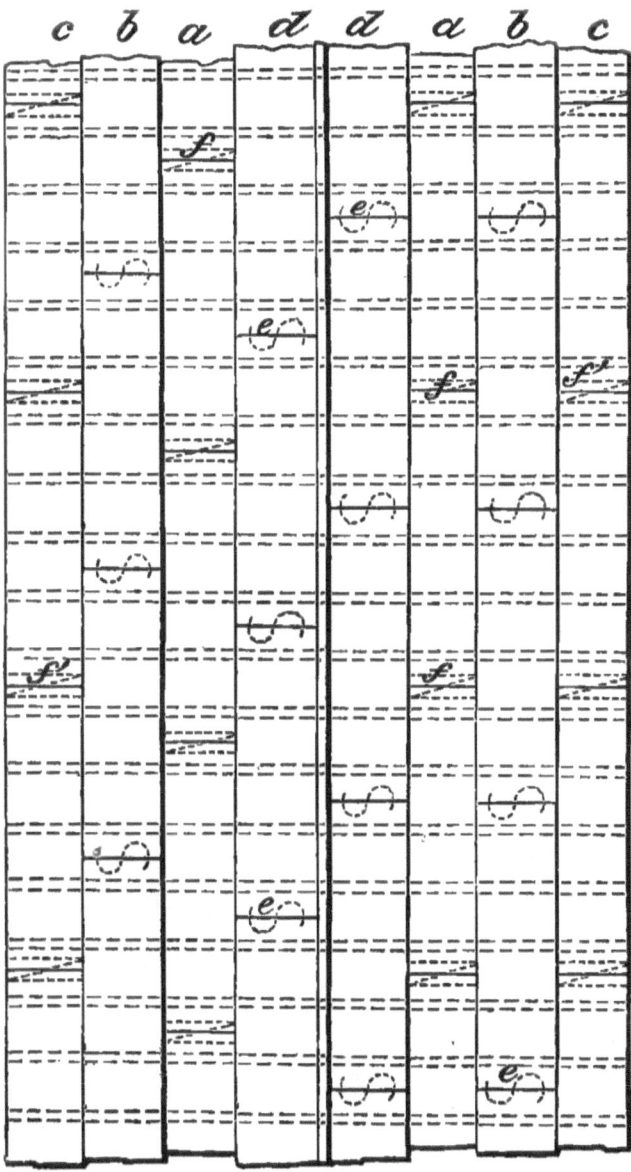

a a. The butts of these go a frame further forward on starboard side (see *ff*).
b b. The butts of these do the same (see *e e e*). *c c.* Butts (see *ff*).
d d. Garboard Strake Butts (see *e e e*).

Outside Plating.—Attention should be paid to having the butts of the garboard strake clear of the scarphs in keel, and that the butts of the garboard plates have three frames between them from the starboard to the port side throughout (Fig. 18).

In order to have the butts of the outside plating a clear two spaces from the bulkheads, have the plates that come in wake of bulkheads a space of frames more in length than the average length of plating.

Have the sides of plates, with the Maker's stamp on, put to the outside of ship, so that the Surveyor may see it, on account of the classification.

In the butts of bilge strakes, if the bilge is at all quick, the edges of the plates should be sheered with a slight curve.

In plating vessels attention should be paid not to put too much weight of plating on the top sides until the garboard bilge and bottom is all plated and riveted.

The holes for rivets in the lower edge of double riveting should be punched as near as possible to the edge of frame

Fig. 19.

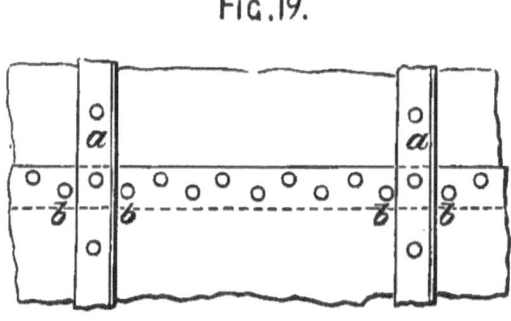

a a. Frames. *b b.* Rivets next frames to be as shown.

(Fig. 19), and spaced, say, for a 3-inch flange and $\frac{3}{4}$-inch rivets, not more than 8 inches pitch.

Have the inside strakes stitched at the butt straps and frames say about six rivets in each butt-strap and two in each frame, before putting on the outside strakes.

The filling-plates at the bulkheads at back of shell-plates

should be at least the width of the fore-and-aft flange of the frame angle-iron longer than two spaces of frames, in the fore-and-aft peake bulkheads, the filling-plates will be about three inches longer on account of the set and bend.

In the plating round the knuckle of stern, see that the plates are kept up to the sheer-marks, and on no account have them below, and allow a clear inch-and-a-quarter from top of rivet-hole to the edge of plate.

In taking off the dimensions to order plates for going round the stern (supposing them to be of average size) an allowance

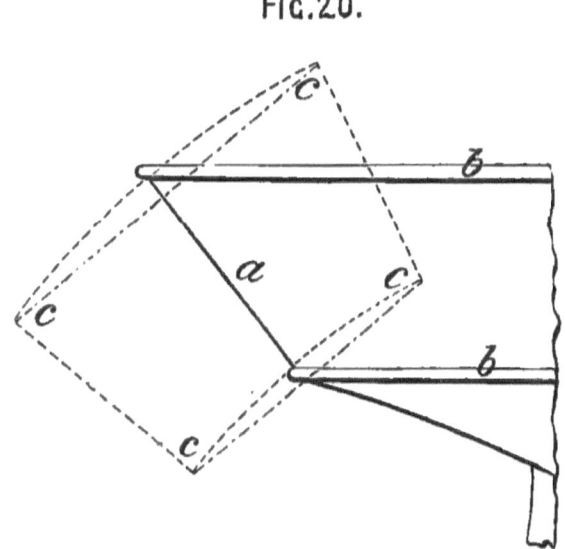

FIG. 20.

a, Centre of plate.   *b b*. Mouldings.
c c c. Development of plate showing allowance.

of about five inches should be made beyond what the plate measures in the depth of the stern (Fig. 20).

In marking the rivet-holes for sheerstrakes aft, attention should be paid to having the holes for connecting the stringer-plate to the shell of the vessel high enough up for the rivet-hole to come in the centre of the flange of the angle-iron (Fig. 21).

In the plating of topgallant forecastles, the plate that is cut for the knightheads should project say about three inches beyond

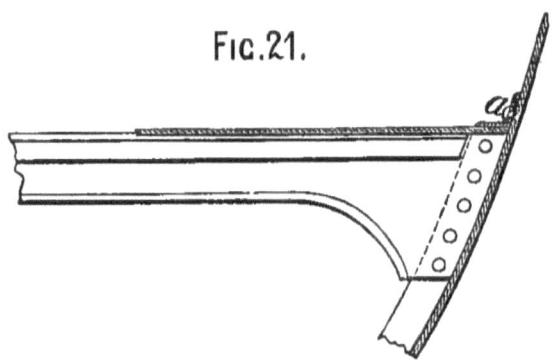

Fig. 21.

a. See that this rivet is not too low in bosom of angle-iron.

the knighthead bulkhead, and the rivets through the bulkhead should be flush on the forward side. The projection is to allow for bolting on the knee-brackets, &c.

Fig. 22 (on next page) is a sketch showing a good arrangement of rivets in frames, heel-pieces, and butt-straps, of garboard-strake.

Fig. 22.

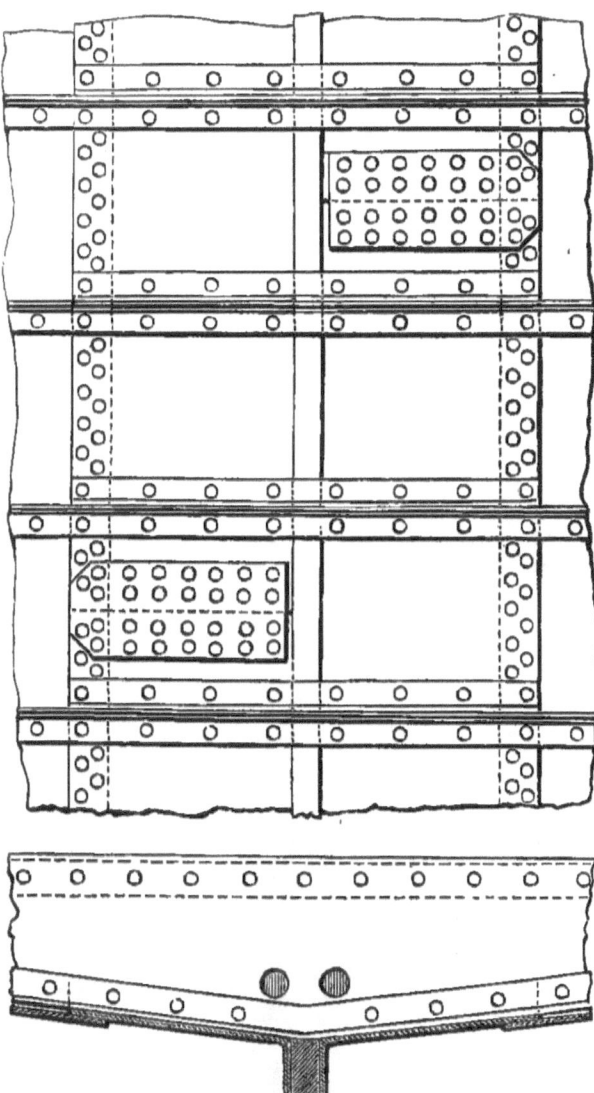

PART II.

Weight per Foot of various sized Plate and Bulb Iron-beams, with two Angle-irons on upper edge, and including Rivets.

One foot of beam-iron $8'' \times \frac{3}{8}''$, with bulb on the lower edge and two angle-irons on the upper edge $3'' \times 2\frac{1}{2}'' \times \frac{3}{8}''$, and two $\frac{5}{8}''$ rivets, weighed 27 lbs.

One foot of plate-iron beam $5'' \times \frac{5}{16}''$, with two angle-irons on the upper edge $1\frac{3}{4}'' \times 1\frac{3}{4}'' \times \frac{3}{16}''$, and two $\frac{1}{2}''$ rivets, weighed 10 lbs. 6 oz.

One foot of plate-iron beam $4\frac{1}{2}'' \times \frac{1}{4}''$, with two angle-irons on the upper edge $2'' \times 2'' \times \frac{1}{4}''$, and two $\frac{1}{2}''$ rivets, weighed 9 lbs. 9 oz.

One foot of plate-iron beam $4'' \times \frac{1}{4}''$, with two angle-irons on the upper edge $1\frac{3}{4}'' \times 1\frac{3}{4}'' \times \frac{3}{16}''$, and two $\frac{1}{2}''$ rivets, weighed 7 lbs. 8¼ oz.

Weight per Yard of Rivets of various Sizes, eighteen Rivets to the Yard.

					lbs.	oz.
1 yard $\frac{3}{4}''$ rivets	....	$2\frac{3}{4}''$ long	....	weighed	8	4
Ditto	....	$2\frac{1}{2}''$,,	....	,,	7	12
Ditto	....	$2\frac{1}{4}''$,,	....	,,	7	8
1 yard $\frac{5}{8}''$ rivets	....	$2\frac{1}{4}''$,,	....	,,	5	8
Ditto	....	$2''$,,	....	,,	5	0
Ditto	....	$1\frac{3}{4}''$,,	....	,,	4	8
1 yard $\frac{1}{2}''$ rivets	....	$\frac{7}{8}''$,,	....	,,	1	8
Ditto	....	$1''$,,	....	,,	1	14
Ditto	....	$1\frac{1}{4}''$,,	....	,,	2	3
Ditto	....	$1\frac{1}{2}''$,,	....	,,	2	6¾
Ditto	....	$2''$,,	....	,,	3	2
1 yard $\frac{3}{8}''$ rivets	....	$1''$,,	....	,,	1	2
Ditto	....	$1\frac{1}{4}''$,,	....	,,	1	3
Ditto	....	$1\frac{1}{2}''$,,	....	,,	1	4

Weight per Yard of Rivets of various Sizes, &c.—continued.

				lbs.	oz.
1 yard $\frac{3}{4}''$ rivets	....	$1\frac{1}{4}''$ long	.... weighed	4	14
Ditto	....	$1\frac{1}{2}''$ „	.... „	5	8
Ditto	....	$1\frac{3}{4}''$ „	.... „	6	7
Ditto	....	$2''$ „	.... „	6	14
Ditto	....	$3''$ „	.... „	8	14
Ditto	....	$3\frac{1}{4}''$ „	.... „	9	2
Ditto	....	$3\frac{1}{2}''$ „	.... „	9	9
1 yard $\frac{7}{8}''$ rivets	....	$2''$ „	.... „	10	12

Weights of various Deck Screws, Deck Bolts, Nails, Rooves, Dumps, Copper Bolts, &c.

One dozen of $\frac{1}{2}''$ deck screws, 3 ins. long, with square heads, weighed 4 lbs. 8 oz.

One dozen of $\frac{1}{2}''$ screw bolts, $3\frac{1}{2}$ ins. long, with cheese heads and nuts, weighed 5 lbs. $6\frac{1}{4}$ oz.

One dozen of $\frac{5}{8}''$ screw bolts, 4 ins. long, with cheese heads and nuts, weighed 8 lbs. $6\frac{1}{4}$ oz.

One dozen of $\frac{3}{4}''$ screw bolts, 9 ins. long, with cheese heads and nuts, weighed 21 lbs. $9\frac{1}{2}$ oz.

One dozen of $\frac{3}{4}''$ screw bolts, 15 ins. long, with nuts, weighed 28 lbs. $12\frac{3}{4}$ oz.

One dozen of 6″ spike nails, weighed 2 lbs. 10 oz.

One dozen of 5″ spike nails, weighed 1 lb. 10 oz.

One dozen of 6″ fine knee nails, weighed 1 lb.

One thousand of round copper rooves, fit for cutters, weighed from $2\frac{1}{2}$ lbs. to 3 lbs.

One thousand of small copper rooves, fit for gigs, weighed 14 oz.

One dozen of metal dumps, $9'' \times \frac{5}{8}''$, weighed 10 lbs. 2 oz.

One dozen of metal dumps, $8'' \times \frac{5}{8}''$, weighed 7 lbs. 9 oz.

One dozen of metal dumps, $6'' \times \frac{1}{2}''$, weighed 4 lbs. 11 oz.

One cwt. of metal nails should be allowed for every 100 sheets of copper of ordinary size.

Weight of One Foot of Copper Bolt.

Diam.	lbs. oz.		Diam.	lbs. oz.
$\tfrac{1}{2}''$	0 12		$\tfrac{7}{8}''$	2 7
$\tfrac{5}{8}''$	1 3		$1''$	3 3
$\tfrac{3}{4}''$	1 12		$1\tfrac{1}{8}''$	4 0

Result of Experiment with Three Pieces of Ship's Beams.

One piece of plate-iron beam 18 ft. long, 10 ins. × ½ in., with two angle irons on the upper edge 3½″ × 3″ × $\tfrac{7}{16}$″, secured to the plate by thirteen ¾″ rivets, required a pressure in the centre of eight and a-half tons to break it.

Weight of beam, 5 cwt. 1 qr. 25 lbs.

One piece of beam 18 ft. long, 10 ins. × ½ in., with bulb on the lower edge, and two angle irons on the upper edge 3½″ × 3″ × $\tfrac{7}{16}$″, secured to the beam by thirteen ¾″ rivets, required a pressure in the centre of ten and a-half tons to break it.

Weight of beam, 6 cwt. 0 qr. 24 lbs.

One piece of plate-iron beam 18 ft. long, 10 ins. × ½ in., with two angle irons on the upper edge 3½″ × 3″ $\tfrac{7}{16}$″, and two angle irons on the lower edge 3″ × 2½″ × $\tfrac{3}{8}$″, secured to the beam by thirteen ¾″ rivets in each edge, required a pressure in the centre of sixteen and a-half tons to break it.

Weight of beam, 7 cwt. 3 qrs. 2 lbs.

Strength and Weight of Flax Canvas.

Weight of One Bolt.

No. 1.	39 yds.	46 lbs.
,, 2.	,,	43 ,,
,, 3.	,,	40 ,,
,, 4.	,,	36 ,,
,, 5.	,,	33 ,,
,, 6.	,,	30 ,,

Breaking Strain of Pieces 1 in. wide, if of good quality.

	Weft.	Warp.
No. 1.	450 lbs.	320 lbs.
,, 2.	420 ,,	300 ,,
,, 3.	400 ,,	280 ,,
,, 4.	380 ,,	260 ,,
,, 5.	350 ,,	230 ,,
,, 6.	330 ,,	220 ,,

Weight of Rivets of different Lengths, $\frac{3}{4}''$ diam.

Number	Size	Weight
100 rivets	$1\frac{1}{2}'' \times \frac{3}{4}''$	weighed 34·42 lbs.
Ditto	$1\frac{5}{8}''$,,	,, 36·25 ,,
Ditto	$1\frac{3}{4}''$,,	,, 37·09 ,,
Ditto	$1\frac{7}{8}''$,,	,, 38·75 ,,
Ditto	$2''$,,	,, 41·50 ,,
Ditto	$2\frac{1}{8}''$,,	,, 42·81 ,,
Ditto	$2\frac{1}{4}''$,,	,, 44·12 ,,
Ditto	$2\frac{3}{8}''$,,	,, 46·84 ,,
Ditto	$2\frac{1}{2}''$,,	,, 48·13 ,,
Ditto	$2\frac{5}{8}''$,,	,, 49·39 ,,
Ditto	$2\frac{3}{4}''$,,	,, 50·66 ,,
Ditto	$2\frac{7}{8}''$,,	,, 51·93 ,,
Ditto	$3''$,,	,, 53·20 ,,
Ditto	$1\frac{3}{8}'' \times \frac{5}{8}''$	,, 21·09 ,,

Weights of $\frac{1}{2}''$ and $\frac{3}{8}''$ Rivets.

Rivets.	Diam.	Length.	cwt.	qrs.	lbs.
1000	$\frac{1}{2}''$	$\frac{3}{4}''$	0	3	6
1000	$\frac{1}{2}''$	$1''$	0	3	16
1000	$\frac{1}{2}''$	$1\frac{1}{4}''$	0	3	26
1000	$\frac{1}{2}''$	$1\frac{1}{2}''$	1	0	15
1000	$\frac{1}{2}''$	$1\frac{3}{4}''$	1	1	0
1000	$\frac{1}{2}''$	$2''$	1	1	20
2891	$\frac{3}{8}''$	$\frac{5}{8}''$	1	0	0
2336	$\frac{3}{8}''$	$\frac{7}{8}''$	1	0	0

Average Allowance for Waste on Converting Timber for Ship-Building Purposes.

English Oak	200 per cent.
English Elm	200 ,,
Yellow Pine, when cut for decks	10 ,,
Yellow Pine, when cut for head and stern work	200 ,,
Dantzic Fir, when cut from planks	10 ,,
Teak	15 ,,
Dantzic Oak	50 ,,
African Oak	100 ,,
Mahogany	30 ,,
American Elm	15 ,,
Quebec Oak	10 ,,
English Oak Plank	50 ,,
Dantzic Fir Plank	25 ,,
Dantzic Oak Plank	40 ,,
Pitch Pine	50 ,,
Greenheart	25 ,,

About 15 per cent. waste on wood materials for joiner work.

Cost per Gallon of various Paints, and the Number of Square Yards each will cover.

Colour.	Per Gallon.	Sq. yds.
Priming	6s. 0d.	55
White	7s. 0d.	44
Lead Colour	6s. 0d.	55
Black	5s. 6d.	90
Stone Colour	7s. 6d.	44
Yellow	6s. 0d.	44
Blue	8s. 6d.	55
Green	6s. 0d.	55
Emerald Green	12s. 0d.	25
Bronze Green	7s. 0d.	60

TABLE of WEIGHTS of LINEAL FEET of ANGLE IRON, EQUAL SIDED.

Size in Inches.	Thick $\frac{1}{4}''$.	Thick $\frac{5}{16}''$.	Thick $\frac{3}{8}''$.	Thick $\frac{7}{16}''$.	Thick $\frac{1}{2}''$.	Thick $\frac{9}{16}''$.	Thick $\frac{5}{8}''$.	Thick $\frac{11}{16}''$.	Thick $\frac{3}{4}''$.
$1\frac{1}{4} \times 1\frac{1}{4}$	2·0	2·62	3·13	3·65	4·2				
$1\frac{3}{8} \times 1\frac{3}{8}$	2·3	2·93	3·44	4·0	4·58				
$1\frac{1}{2} \times 1\frac{1}{2}$	2·5	3·13	3·75	4·38	5·01				
$1\frac{5}{8} \times 1\frac{5}{8}$	2·71	3·39	4·0	4·74	5·43				
$1\frac{3}{4} \times 1\frac{3}{4}$	2·92	3·65	4·37	5·11	5·85				
$1\frac{7}{8} \times 1\frac{7}{8}$	3·13	3·9	4·68	5·48	6·26				
2×2	3·34	4·17	5·0	5·84	6·6				
$2\frac{1}{4} \times 2\frac{1}{4}$	3·77	4·7	5·56	6·57	7·51				
$2\frac{1}{2} \times 2\frac{1}{2}$	4·17	5·26	6·25	7·30	8·36				
$2\frac{3}{4} \times 2\frac{3}{4}$	4·5	5·5	6·87	8·02	9·2				
3×3	5·0	6·26	7·51	8·8	10·06	11·36	12·6	13·85	15·01
$3\frac{1}{4} \times 3\frac{1}{4}$	5·42	6·78	8·13	9·48	10·82	12·20	13·56	14·98	16·31
$3\frac{1}{2} \times 3\frac{1}{2}$	5·8	7·3	8·8	10·25	11·68	13·15	14·62	16·12	17·6
$3\frac{3}{4} \times 3\frac{3}{4}$	6·26	7·85	9·36	10·96	12·55	14·1	15·64	17·7	18·74
4×4	6·61	8·38	10·14	11·85	13·37	15·5	16·73	18·55	20·31
$4\frac{1}{4} \times 4\frac{1}{4}$	7·01	8·81	10·61	12·4	14·18	15·9	17·62	19·45	21·22
$4\frac{1}{2} \times 4\frac{1}{2}$	7·51	9·48	11·31	13·18	15·04	17·0	18·8	20·7	22·6
$4\frac{3}{4} \times 4\frac{3}{4}$	7·76	9·8	11·81	13·82	15·83	17·75	19·61	21·68	23·7
5×5	8·35	10·5	12·54	14·65	16·75	18·85	20·89	23·0	25·08
$5\frac{1}{4} \times 5\frac{1}{4}$	8·75	11·0	13·17	15·4	17·55	20·0	21·92	24·15	26·34
$5\frac{1}{2} \times 5\frac{1}{2}$	9·18	11·5	13·78	16·06	18·35	20·78	23·0	25·35	27·63
$5\frac{3}{4} \times 5\frac{3}{4}$	9·61	12·0	14·4	16·8	19·2	21·6	24·0	26·38	28·76
6×6	10·13	12·75	15·3	17·75	20·13	22·9	25·42	28·0	30·6

To ascertain the weight of unequal sided angle iron, add the length of the two sides together and divide it. *Example*, to find the weight of angle iron $4 \times 3 \times \frac{3}{8}$, refer to Table for $3\frac{1}{2} \times 3\frac{1}{2} \times \frac{3}{8}$, giving 8·8 lbs. per lineal foot.

Weights of One Fathom of Chain Cable of various sizes.

Ins.	lbs.	Ins.	lbs.	Ins.	lbs.
$\frac{5}{16}$	5½	$\frac{7}{8}$	43	$1\frac{7}{16}$	115
$\frac{3}{8}$	8	$\frac{15}{16}$	50	$1\frac{1}{2}$	125
$\frac{7}{16}$	11	1	58	$1\frac{5}{8}$	145
$\frac{1}{2}$	14	$1\frac{1}{16}$	66	$1\frac{3}{4}$	163
$\frac{9}{16}$	18	$1\frac{1}{8}$	72	$1\frac{7}{8}$	190
$\frac{5}{8}$	26	$1\frac{3}{16}$	80	2	224
$\frac{11}{16}$	30	$1\frac{1}{4}$	86	$2\frac{1}{8}$	246
$\frac{3}{4}$	34	$1\frac{5}{16}$	96	$2\frac{1}{4}$	262
$\frac{13}{16}$	38	$1\frac{3}{8}$	108		

The above weights will vary somewhat according to the Makers, but may be used as an average in estimating for cost and displacements.

Number of Cubic Feet usually allowed in Chain Lockers for 100 Fathoms of Chain.

Ins.	ft.	Ins.	ft.	Ins.	ft.
$\frac{3}{4}$	16	$1\frac{1}{4}$	50	$1\frac{5}{8}$	80
$\frac{7}{8}$	22	$1\frac{3}{8}$	60	$1\frac{3}{4}$	92
1	30	$1\frac{1}{2}$	70	$1\frac{7}{8}$	105
$1\frac{1}{8}$	40				

Weights of One Cubic Foot of Timber, the Result of Experiments weighing the Logs when Wet and when Seasoned, taking the Mean.

	lbs.	oz.		lbs.	oz.
Dantzic Fir	37	4	Red Pine	41	3
African Oak	64	8	Riga Fir	46	8
Sabicu	69	12	Memel Fir	35	4
American Elm	43	0	White Deal	42	8
English Oak	56	4	Yellow Pine	34	4
Dantzic Oak	47	8	English Elm	43	8
Canada Oak	44	4	Mahogany	39	8
Italian Oak	61	8	Teak	46	8
Belgian Oak	56	0	Malabar Teak	53	0
Pitch Pine	41	4	Poon	57	4
Cedar	48	0	Beech	43	8
Larch	33	8	Ash	47	8

Formulæ for finding the approximate Gross Register Tonnage.

$\dfrac{L \times B \times D}{100} \times \cdot 7$ full form sailing vessels.

Ditto $\times \cdot 65$ clipper form and two decks.
Ditto $\times \cdot 68$ clipper form and three decks.
Ditto $\times \cdot 5$ sharp yachts.

L represents length from inside of stem to fore side of stern-post, measured on upper deck. B represents inside breadth. D represents depth from top of floors to the underside of deck, measured amidships.

Note.—For a deep sailing-vessel with flat floor, carried well fore and aft, the multiplier will in some cases be ·75; but this is for an extra burthensome vessel.

Formulæ for approximating the Weight of Outside Plating of Iron Sailing Ships of the usual Class.

For the A *a* class, multiply the builder's tonnage by ·19.
  „ A *b* „   „   „   ·165.

Iron ships are from 10 to 15 per cent. lighter than wooden vessels.

Rates of Wages per Day of the various Trades engaged in Shipbuilding Establishments in the following Ports of the United Kingdom:—

THAMES.

	s.	d.		s.	d.
Shipwrights, 1st Class	7	0	Strikers	4	0
„ 2nd „	6	0	Caulkers (Wood)	6	6
Joiners	5	6	Sawyers	5	6
Blacksmiths, 1st Class	6	6	Boat-builders	6	0
„ 2nd „	6	0	Riggers, 1st Class	5	6
Platers, 1st Class	7	0	„ 2nd „	5	0
„ 2nd „	6	0	Angle-iron Smiths	6	6
Drillers	3	8	Chippers	5	0
Helpers	3	6	Holders-up	4	0
Screwers	3	0	Rivet-boys	1	0
Riveters	5	0	Labourers, 1st Class	3	6
Caulkers (Iron)	5	0	Plumbers	6	6
Labourers	3	0	Labourer (Head)	4	6

Painters, 6½*d.* to 8*d.* per hour. Red-lead Hands, 4*d.* to 5*d.* per hour. Grainers, 6*s.* to 10*s.* per day.

MERSEY.

	s.	d.		s.	d.
Shipwrights	7	0	Labourers, 2nd Class	3	4
Joiners	5	6	Painters	5	6
Blacksmiths	6	0	Strikers	4	0
Platers (in the yards)	6	0	Engineers, 1st Class	6	0
„ (in the docks)	7	0	„ 2nd „	5	0
Riveters (in the yards)	4	8	Drillers	3	4
„ (in the docks)	5	8	Platers' helpers	3	0
Labourers, 1st Class	4	0			

Men working in the docks at the North End are usually paid a trifle extra.

WEAR AND TYNE.

	s.	d.		s.	d.
Shipwrights	5	0	Riveters	4	2
Joiners	4	6	Labourers	2	10
Blacksmiths, 1st Class	4	6	Painters, 1st Class	4	6
,, 2nd ,,	4	4	,, 2nd ,,	4	2
Platers, 1st Class	4	6	Carvers	5	0
,, 2nd ,,	4	2			

CLYDE.

	s.	d.		s.	d.
Shipwrights	4	6	Mechanics, 2nd Class	4	0
Joiners, 1st Class	4	10	Fitters, 1st Class	4	2
,, 2nd ,,	4	2	,, 2nd ,,	3	4
Blacksmiths, 1st Class	4	8	Fitters' helpers, 1st Class	2	4
,, 2nd ,,	4	0	,, 2nd ,,	2	2
Platers, 1st Class	4	8	Labourers	2	6
,, 2nd ,,	4	0	Painters	5	0
Riveters, 1st Class	3	6	Red-leaders, 1st Class	2	10
,, 2n ,,	3	4	,, 2nd ,,	2	6
Holders-up	2	6	Plumbers	5	0
Rivet-boys	1	1	Boat-builders	4	6
Drillers, 1st Class	3	0	Riggers, 1st Class	4	6
,, 2nd ,,	2	6	,, 2nd ,,	4	2
Helpers, 1st ,,	3	4	Blockmakers, 1st Class	4	6
Helpers, 2nd ,,	1	10	,, 2nd ,,	4	0
Caulkers (Iron), 1st Class	3	6	Machine Saw-workers, 1st Class	5	4
,, ,, 2nd ,,	3	0	,, ,, 2nd ,,	2	10
Strikers	2	10	Carvers, 1st Class	4	8
Mechanics, 1st Class	4	8	,, 2nd ,,	4	0

SHIPWRIGHTS' WORK.

East Coast of England.

Contract for the Work on an Iron Sailing-ship,
$220 \times 37 \times 25 = 1440$ *Tons.*

	£	s.	d.
Laying main deck ready for caulking	61	5	0
Forecastle ditto and covering boards	13	0	0
Lower ,, ,,	57	0	0
Ceiling main hold	70	15	0
Fillings on main deck	7	0	0
Main rail and pin rail	19	0	0
Waterways on main deck	18	10	0
,, lower ditto and fillings	18	0	0
Topgallant rail and bulwarks round stern	5	10	0
Topsail sheet bitts and mooring bitts, with fife rail	8	5	0
Fitting and fastening two capstans and two winches	5	0	0
Chain-lockers with pipe and hatchway	10	0	0
Battening main hold, tween decks and bulkheads	39	10	0
Sole and side-pieces in front of topgallant forecastle	3	10	0
Hawse pipes, fitting inside and outside	10	0	0
Laying cabin deck	7	15	0
Ceiling afterhold, forepeake, and forecastle	20	0	0
Fitting iron stanchions on the forecastle deck	1	5	0
Fife rail in front of topgallant forecastle and stanchions	1	15	0
Ceiling cabin and forecastle with 1¼-in. pine	19	10	0
Head, head rails, and fitting all carved work	15	3	0
Fitting bowsprit bearers and saddle	4	0	0
Wedging masts and fitting steps to mizen masts	3	0	0
Fitting and fastening all timber heads	3	15	0
Fitting and fastening all mast combings	4	0	0
Building up pump well	3	5	0
Laying the fore and after peake decks	8	0	0
Fitting and fastening combings for houses on main deck	3	0	0
Sundry jobs about decks	6	0	0
	£446	13	0

Laying the keel-block, shoring, ribanding, and caulking not included in the above estimate.

Contract for the Work on an Iron Screw Steam-vessel,
$215 \times 30 \times 17 = 943$ *Tons.*

	£	s.	d.
Laying main deck ready for caulking	36	0	0
Poop deck ditto	9	10	0
Cabin deck ditto	9	5	0
Forecastle deck ditto	6	10	0
Ceiling main hold	15	15	0
Ceiling fore hold	16	10	0
Covering all tanks	6	10	0
Ceiling coal-bunkers	7	15	0
Fitting and fastening main deck waterways	6	10	0
Ditto poop covering boards	5	15	0
,, forecastle	4	10	0
,, hawsepipes, &c.	6	0	0
,, all mouldings and rails	7	15	0
,, figure-head and carving	8	0	0
,, boiler bearers, chocks, &c.	7	0	0
All ceiling in engine-room and about boilers	3	10	0
Knightheads, bowsprit bearer, and saddle	3	0	0
Topgallant bulwarks round stern with rail	4	10	0
Chain-lockers and pipes	5	15	0
Wedging bowsprit and masts	1	10	0
Clog for pumps, fitting ditto, and casing-in pumps	2	5	0
Fitting companion and skylight, main rail and pin rails with pins	8	5	0
Fitting and fastening all timber heads, bevels and fair leaders	3	5	0
Framing and laying deck of deck-house, 20 feet long	20	0	0
Fitting and fastening iron stanchions on poop and forecastle	5	10	0
Fitting and fastening sole and side pieces on front of forecastle	3	5	0
Fife rail and stanchions for front of forecastle and poop	3	10	0
Bolting 2 winches and capstan	1	10	0
Ditto and fitting windlass	8	5	0
Cathead chocks, stoppers, &c.	2	0	0
Filling on main deck beneath forecastle and waterways	6	0	0
Battens in main and fore holds and tween decks	11	10	0
Mast combings, &c.	1	15	0
Launching and lifting ways	40	0	0
	£288	10	0
Contract for shoring, ribanding, and laying blocks	£63	15	0

Shipwrights' Work on Launching an Iron Sailing-ship of 1000 *Tons.*

Laying the ways and all work connected therewith, replacing the ways in yard, and all wood, &c., connected therewith, in their proper places on the premises and to the entire satisfaction of the foreman appointed. (Unforeseen occurrences in launching. excepted.) For the sum of £40. 10s. sterling.

THAMES DISTRICT.

Contract for the following Work on an Iron Paddle-steamer,
200 × 2'6 6" × 14' 6" = 687 *Tons* :—

	£	s.	d.
Laying blocks	9	0	0
Putting ship in frame, ribanding, &c.	47	0	0
Making staging	32	10	0
Waterways, combings, laying the deck, and lining off strakes	82	0	0
Roughtree timbers, timber heads, planksheer, and roughtree rail complete	45	0	0
Head, with hawsepipes, &c., all complete	15	0	0
Fitting windlass	10	10	0
Paddle-boxes, all complete	48	0	0
Stern, taffrail, pipes, carved work, and steerage	24	10	0
Fittings in engine-room and attending engineers with men ..	25	0	0
Launching	40	0	0
Fitting boats' davits, awning, stancheons, catheads, &c.	9	0	0
Lower decks	26	0	0
Futling in the fore and after holds	31	0	0
Lining plates and getting in battens	16	0	0
Making moulds about vessel	9	10	0
Shifting the ribands, attending to shores, &c.	20	0	0
Wedging masts, bowsprit, fitting shroud plates for rigging, cleats, eye-bolts, &c.	7	10	0
Making chain-box for cable, and fitting iron work to ditto ..	2	0	0
Fitting gangway ladders, cranes, platforms, &c.	8	0	0
Sundry work about decks and holds	20	0	0
Store-rooms, scuttle hatches, &c.	14	0	0
	£541	10	0

The cost of the above work is for the ordinary type of Passenger Channel Steamers, built in the Thames yards.

Contract for the following Work on an Iron Screw-steamer,
$225 \times 30' \; 6'' \times 22 = 1023$ *Tons.*

	£	s.	d.
Laying blocks	11	0	0
Ribanding and stages	90	0	0
Making all moulds..	30	0	0
Shifting shores and attending iron workers	48	0	0
Upper deck, roughtrees, planksheer rails, combings, &c. ..	225	0	0
Stern and steerage	47	10	0
Fitting windlass	19	0	0
Head, with hawsepipes, &c., all complete	26	10	0
Futling, &c., in holds	120	0	0
Bulkheads	21	0	0
Launching	56	0	0
Berthing	18	0	0
Channels, and fitting all iron work	30	0	0
Lower decks	45	0	0
Boats' davits, awning-stancheons, catheads, &c.	13	10	0
Wedging masts and bowsprit, and fitting cleats, pin-racks, &c.	15	0	0
Fitting gangway ladders, &c.	11	10	0
Sundries about decks, &c.	33	0	0
Fittings in engine-room and attending engineers with men ..	36	0	0
Store-rooms, scuttles, &c.	26	10	0
	£922	10	0

The above is the cost of labour on an Ocean-going Passenger Steamer with a spar-deck.

CLYDE DISTRICT.

Cost of the Shipwrights' Work on an Iron Screw-steamer, $245 \times 30 \times 20 = 1063$ *Tons. Half-poop* 60 *feet long, topgallant forecastle, and house amidships.*

	£	s.	d.
Waterways	64	0	0
Decks	80	0	0
Hatches	107	0	0
Ceiling	80	0	0
Rails	29	0	0
Masts and spars	32	0	0
Carried forward	£392	0	0

	£	s.	d.
Brought forward	392	0	0
Bowsprit	12	0	0
Fenders	3	0	0
Mooring bitts	6	0	0
Mouldings at stern	7	0	0
Scuppers	9	0	0
Bulwarks	21	0	0
Catheads	7	0	0
Launch	41	0	0
Shores and ribanding	67	0	0
	£565	0	0

Shipwrights' Work on an Iron Passenger Paddle-steamer, 260 × 35 × 18 = 1557 tons, fitted with deck houses, all fore and aft, wooden bulwarks, teak decks, &c. Cost £1030.

Prices paid for Laying Decks.

The plank to be carried on board, laid, dowelled, and bolted, ready for caulking.

Price per Lineal Foot.

	d.		d.
5″ × 4″	$\frac{3}{4}$	6″ × 4″	1
5″ × 3″	$\frac{1}{2}$	6″ × 3″	$\frac{3}{4}$

The Allowance made by Shipwrights for Apprentices when they take Work by Contract.

Year.	Rate per Day.	Stop for each Apprentice.
	s. d.	s. d.
1st	1 0	Nil
2nd	1 2	1 6
3rd	1 4	1 9
4th	1 6	2 0
5th	1 8	3 0
6th	2 0	3 6
7th	2 4	4 6

The above rates refer to the Thames.

CAULKERS' WORK.

Thames.

	s.	d.
9" plank per 100 feet	17	0
8" ,, ,,	16	0
7" ,, ,,	15	0
6" ,, ,,	14	0
5" ,, ,,	13	0
4" ,, ,,	12	6
3" ,, ,,	10	6
2½" reamed ,,	8	6
2½" not reamed ,,	6	6
2" ,, ,,	5	6
1½" ,, ,,	5	0
Paint-work ,,	7	0
Oak decks, reamed and horsed down	7	0
Ditto, not horsed down	6	0
Fir decks, reamed	5	0
Ditto, not reamed	4	0
Old decks	3	0

BOAT BUILDING.

Cost of Five Ship's Boats of the following Dimensions, built and fitted in accordance with the Board of Trade Regulations for Steam-vessels carrying Passengers:—

Planking Yellow Pine.

2 lifeboats	24' × 6' 9"	× 2' 8"	
1 cutter	24' × 6' 3"	× 2' 8"	
1 gig	24' × 5' 4"	× 2' 4"	
1 dingy	16' × 4' 6"	× 2' 3"	

	£	s.	d.
½" pine plank	2	11	8
⅝" elm, birch, and pine	9	8	1
¾" elm, birch, and pine	1	11	10
2" elm	2	8	8
Carried forward	£16	0	3

	£	s.	d.
Brought forward	16	0	3
1¾" elm	0	4	3
1¾" oak and elm slabs	0	7	10½
2¼" elm plank	0	19	0
¾" elm slabs	0	3	6
⅞" elm slabs	0	5	0
1⅛" elm slabs	0	3	4
Round oak ends	0	10	0
Larch roots	0	17	6
1½" pine slabs	0	1	10
1" pine plank	0	8	4
1" mahogany plank	0	6	0
1½" birch plank	0	6	0
2¼" oak plank	0	7	6
Ash oars	5	14	4
Stem and keel plates	1	2	6
Thole-pins, plates, &c.	0	5	10
Boat-hooks	0	6	3
Rudder-bands	0	12	6
Ring-bolts and eye-bolts	1	0	0
Brass work	0	13	1½
Brass screws	0	0	6
Wrought-copper nails	0	12	0½
Cut-copper nails	1	19	4½
Copper rooves	0	6	0
Iron-plate nails	0	0	10
Copper tacks	0	1	1½
Iron nails	0	9	4
Sand-paper	0	0	8½
Brass chain	0	0	3½
Iron chain	0	0	4
Green-heart thole-pins	0	5	0
Wooden plugs	0	0	9
1 buoyant apparatus	1	10	0
Knee-bolts	0	1	9
Washers	0	0	9
Round iron	0	2	6
Boat-builders' wages	37	0	0
Painting	4	10	0
	£77	16	2½

Boatbuilders' wages per foot length of boats, taking the cost as the same for each; but the lifeboats are actually more costly than the others .. 0 6 7¼

Cost of a Boat suitable for a small Coasting Vessel, 15' 6" × 5' 0" × 2' 3".

	£	s.	d.
Elm plank slabs and rinds	0	11	7½
Oak pieces and rinds	0	5	6½
Iron bolts	0	0	8
Iron nails (wrought)	0	1	4
Iron nails (cut)	0	0	1½
Small bolts and washers	0	0	3½
Copper tacks	0	0	4½
Oakum	0	0	7
Sand-paper	0	0	2
Copper nails	0	10	6
Pitch pine slabs	0	3	8
1" pine plank	0	4	0
Larch planking	0	15	0
½" pine rinds	0	3	0
Breast-hooks	0	2	0
Beam-knees	0	4	0
Ring-bolts	0	1	9
Boat-builders' wages	2	12	0
Oars	0	11	4
	£6	7	11½
Boat-builders' wages per foot length of boat, for this class, about	0	3	8

Cost of a Diagonally-built Ship's Boat, planked with two Thicknesses of Teak or Mahogany, each $\frac{5}{16}$" thick in the side, and $\frac{3}{5}$" in the bottom. All Copper-fastened, and fitted in first style. 26' 6" × 7" × 3'.

	£	s.	d.
Materials	33	17	0
Wages	18	10	0
	£52	7	0

London Prices for Iron Work paid in the generality of the Thames Building Yards.

Plating, smith work, and riveting girder work, complete, £3. 5s. per ton weight.

Plating alone, £1. 15s. per ton.

Cylinder boiler work, finished, about £4. 7s. 6d. to £4. 12s. 6d. per ton.

Engine and paddle beams, plating, and smith work, £3. 5s. per ton.

Angular tanks, including caulking, 6d. per yard; square tanks, 4½d. per yard.

Water tue-irons, 10d. per lb.

Plating per Ton.

Thickness.	Per ton. £ s. d.	Thickness.	Per ton. £ s. d.
½"	1 16 0	7/16"	2 1 0
3/8"	2 6 0	5/16"	2 11 0
¼"	2 16 0	3/16"	3 1 0

Outside Riveting—per Yard.

Diameter.	Seams. s. d.	Timbers. s. d.	Diameter.	Keels. s. d.	s. d.
¼"	0 7		1¼"	6 0	and 7 0
7/16"	0 8	0 11	1⅛"	4 6	
½"	0 9	1 1	1"	3 8	
5/8"	0 11	1 3	7/8"	2 4	
¾"	1 3	1 10	3/4"	1 10	
7/8"	1 4	2 4	5/8"	1 6	

Inside Work—per Yard.

Diameter.	s. d.	Diameter.	s. d.
3/8" or 7/16"	0 6	¾"	1 0
½"	0 8	7/8"	1 1
5/8"	0 10		

One yard of rivets of any diameter is eighteen.

Drilling Solids.

Diameter	2"	1¾"	1½"	1¼"	1"	7/8"	3/4"
Per inch	6d.	5d.	4½d.	3½d.	2d.	1½d.	1¼d.

Ripping 3d. per foot.   Chipping seams 1½d. per foot.

Cross-Cutting Plates.

Thickness	1/8"	¼"	3/8"	½"	5/8"	3/4"	7/8"	1'
Per foot	2d.	3d.	4½d.	6d.	7½d.	9d.	10½d.	1s.

Cross-Cutting Lights.

Diameter	12"	9"	8"	7"	6"
Each	2s.	1s. 6d.	1s. 2d.	1s.	10d.

Drilling Lights.

Diameter	12″	9″	8″	7″	6″
Each	2s. 6d.	1s. 9d.	1s. 2d.	10d.	8d.

Fixing Lights.

This includes drilling, countersinking, and making joints.

Diameter	12″	9″	8″	7″	6″
Each	2s.	1s. 6d.	1s. 2d.	1s.	10d.

The general price for drilling, on vessels taking the average, costs $7\frac{1}{2}d.$, but often varies above and under.

Angle-Iron Timbers, &c.

Top or Single Cut.		Middle Cut.	
6″	4d.	6″	5d.
5″	$3\frac{1}{2}d.$	5″	$4\frac{1}{2}d.$
4″	3d.	4″	4d.
3″	$2\frac{1}{2}d.$	3″	$3\frac{1}{2}d.$
2″	$1\frac{1}{2}d.$	2″	2d.

Drilling $1\frac{1}{2}″$ holes	2s. 0d. per dozen.
,, $1\frac{7}{16}″$ and $1\frac{3}{8}″$ holes	1s. 6d. ,,
,, $1\frac{1}{4}″$ and $1\frac{1}{8}″$,,	1s. 3d. ,,

Boiler Drilling.

Diameter.	Per doz.		Diameter.	Per doz.	
	s.	d.		s.	d.
$1\frac{1}{2}″$	2	0	$1\frac{1}{8}″$	1	6
$1\frac{3}{8}″$	1	9	1″	1	3
$1\frac{1}{4}″$	1	9	$\frac{7}{8}″$	1	0
			$\frac{5}{8}″$	0	11

Drilling for and fixing Plumber Work.

		s.	d.
Side closet holes	each	2	0
Water course	,,	1	6
Tank holes	,,	1	6
Alljoints (making)	,,	1	3
Sluice valves	,,	2	6
Kingston cock	,,	2	6
Port lights	,,	2	0
Scupper rings	,,	1	6
Port riddles	,,	2	0
Bulkhead cock	,,	2	6

Sweeping Beam Iron.

	s.	d.
12"	1	0
10"	0	10
8"	0	8
6"	0	6

Putting Together.

	s.	d.
12"	0	11
10"	0	8
8"	0	6
6"	0	5
4½"	0	3½

Sweeping Angle-Iron for Beams.

		s.	d.
20 ft. long	4" × 3½"	0	6
Ditto	3½" × 3"	0	5
Ditto	3" × 3"	0	4
Ditto	2½" × 2"	0	3½

Straightening Angle-Iron Bars.

6" × 4½"	1d. per bar.
5" × 3"	½d. „

Angle-Bars, Bevelled and Bent to Moulds, per foot.

	s.	d.			s.	d.
6" × 4½"	0	3		4" × 3"	0	1½
5" × 3½"	0	2½		3" × 3"	0	1

Bending Timbers (per pair).

		£	s.	d.
7" × 5"	50 ft. long	1	0	0
6" × 4½"	ditto	0	16	0
5" × 3½"	ditto	0	14	0

Shutting Angle-Iron (Plain Shuts).

	s.	d.			s.	d.
6" × 4½"	2	0		4" × 3½"	1	1
7" × 3½"	2	10		3" × 2½"	0	8½
5" × 3½"	1	6		2½" × 2½"	0	7
				2" × 2"	0	4

Shutting Deck Beams (Middle Shut).

	s.	d.			s.	d.
12"	2	11		8"	2	1
10"	2	6		6"	0	10

Angle-Iron Corners.

	s. d.		s. d.
1½"	0 3	5"	1 6
2"	0 5	5½"	1 10
3"	0 9	6"	2 2
4"	1 1	6½"	2 6
4½"	1 3	7"	2 10

Turning Beam Ends, Filling-up, and Shutting.

	s. d.		s. d.		s. d.
10"	2 3	8"	2 1	6"	1 8

Shutting Beams in Middle to Length.

	s. d.		s. d.
6"	1 1	10"	2 4
8"	1 11	12"	3 3

Bending and Fitting-up Beam Ends.

	s. d.		s. d.		s. d.
10"	3 3	8"	2 0	6"	1 4

Plate Joggles—Double, 1s.; Single, 6d.

Shutting Plates.

Width.	s. d.	Width.	s. d.	Width.	s. d.
2"	0 2	10"	1 4	17"	3 0
3"	0 3	11"	1 6	18"	3 2
4"	0 4	12"	1 9	19"	3 6
5"	0 6	13"	2 0	20"	3 10
6"	0 8	14"	2 3	21"	4 2
7"	1 0	15"	2 6	22"	4 10
8"	1 1	16"	2 9	24"	5 6
9"	1 2				

Plate Beams (Middle Shut).

	s. d.		s. d.
12"	2 2	8"	1 4
10"	1 8	6"	0 10

Angle-Iron Joggles.

	s. d.		s. d.
1½"	0 2	4½"	1 0
2"	0 3	5"	1 3
2½"	0 4½	5½"	1 6
3"	0 6	6"	1 10
3½"	0 8	6½"	2 2
4"	0 10	7"	2 6

Prices paid for Iron Work in some of the Thames Yards, differing in various ways from the previous List.

BENDING TIMBERS, PER PAIR.

	s. d.		s. d.
$2\frac{1}{2}'' \times 2\frac{1}{2}'' \times \frac{3}{8}''$	2 6	$3'' \times 3'' \times \frac{3}{8}''$	3 0
$2\frac{1}{2}'' \times 2'' \times \frac{3}{8}''$	2 0	$3\frac{1}{2}'' \times 3'' \times \frac{7}{16}''$	3 4
$3'' \times 2\frac{1}{2}'' \times \frac{3}{8}''$	2 2	$4'' \times 3\frac{1}{2}'' \times \frac{7}{16}''$	3 6

Punching and fixing these frames according to length, 2s. to 3s. per pair.

Price for bending, punching, and fixing on keel, $3\frac{1}{2}'' \times 3'' \times \frac{7}{16}''$, 8s. per pair.

BENDING ONLY.

$6'' \times 4\frac{1}{2}'' \times \frac{1}{2}''$, and $5'' \times 3\frac{1}{2}'' \times \frac{7}{16}''$, 13s. 0d. per pair.
$6'' \times 5\frac{1}{2}'' \times \frac{1}{2}''$, and $5'' \times 3\frac{1}{2}'' \times \frac{1}{2}''$, 14s. 2d.   ,,

Punching and fixing, from 4s. to 5s. 6d. per pair.

PLATING, viz.:—

Punching, Shearing, Fitting, and leaving all ready for Riveters, Strips included.

	s. d.			s. d.	
$\frac{5}{16}''$ Plate	47 0	per ton.	$\frac{3}{8}''$ Plate	38 0	per ton.
$\frac{1}{4}''$,, ...	48 6	,,	$\frac{1}{2}''$,, ...	36 0	,,

MAKING, SWEEPING, FITTING, AND FIXING BEAMS.

10" Bulb iron, with two angle-irons on the top edge, 8d. per foot run.
  8"   Ditto   ditto   6d.   ,,
  6"   Ditto   ditto   5d.   ,,

Angle-iron beams, $5'' \times 3\frac{1}{2}''$, $2\frac{1}{2}d.$ per foot run.

T IRON BEAMS.

	s. d.			s. d.	
$4'' \times 3\frac{1}{2}''$	0 2	per foot.	$3'' \times 3''$	0 $1\frac{1}{2}$	per foot.
$3\frac{1}{2}'' \times 3''$	0 $1\frac{1}{2}$	,,			

SHUTTING ANGLE-IRON.

	s. d.			s. d.	
$6'' \times 4\frac{1}{2}''$	2 0	each shut.	$3'' \times 2\frac{1}{2}''$	0 8	each shut.
$5'' \times 3\frac{1}{2}''$	1 4	,,	$2\frac{1}{2}'' \times 2''$	0 6	,,
$4'' \times 3\frac{1}{2}''$	1 0	,,	$1\frac{1}{2}'' \times 1\frac{1}{2}''$	0 4	,,
$3\frac{1}{2}'' \times 3''$	0 10	,,			

Angle-iron corners the same price as shuts.

BENDING AND FILLING UP BEAM ENDS.

	s. d.			s. d.
10″	2 4 each.		6″	1 2 each.
8″	1 8 ,,			

MIDDLE SHUT IN BEAMS.

	s. d.			s. d.
10″	2 4 each.		6″	1 4 each.
8″	1 10 ,,			

PRICE FOR SHUTTING OR WELDING PLATES.

Width.	s. d.	Width.	s. d.
30″	5 0	12″	1 7
24″	4 10	11″	1 5
22″	4 1	10″	1 3
20″	3 8	9″	1 1
18″	3 1	8″	0 11
17″	2 10	7″	0 8
16″	2 7	6″	0 6
15″	2 4	5″	0 5
14″	2 1	4″	0 4
13″	1 10	3″	0 3

Riveting, per yard, prices the same as in previous list.

CAULKING IRON VESSELS.

	s. d.
Seams, per foot	0 1½
Butts, ,,	0 3½

EAST COAST OF ENGLAND.

Cost of Labour on the Iron Work of a Sailing-vessel of about 500 Tons B.M. built on the 400-ton Scale to Lloyd's A a Class.

	£ s. d.
Frame complete $3\frac{1}{2}″ \times 3″ \times \frac{7}{16}″$	1 2 0
Divided as follows:—	
Turning frame	0 3 6
Punching	0 1 6
Turning reverse frames	0 2 6
Putting on ditto	0 2 6
Turning beams	0 1 6
Turning angle-irons for beams	0 1 6
Finishing beams	0 4 0
Board work, &c.	0 5 0
Per frame	£1 2 0

Frame complete, includes turning the iron frame, setting beams, and reverse angle-irons for frames and beams, punching ditto, fitting floors, and cutting ends of frames to lengths marked on board or mould, and when finished to be placed alongside of keel ready for putting up. Finishing beams, includes cutting to length and to angle, or flare of ship's frame, fitting on the angle-irons, and making all ready for riveting.

For setting up frame in place, on *keel* (about), 4s.

The above includes securing on the floor-plates to frames, beams to frames, and laying across the keel ready for riveting; and after the riveters are finished, canting the frame up and putting in place, also putting on the short lug or junk, piece of double reverse angle-iron in wake of centre keelson. Also the short vertical lug-piece for intercostal keelson. (Shipwrights or Carpenters shore up frames, attend to blocks, and otherwise complete ribanding and keeping fair.)

	£	s.	d.
Shell plates (each)	0	4	9
Keel plates	0	9	3
Main and lower deck stringer plates, about 9 feet long (each)	0	5	0
Angle-iron for ditto (32 feet long)	0	4	6
Poop and forecastle angle bars	0	5	0
,, plates	0	5	6
Intercostal keelson plates	0	1	0
Angle bars for centre keelson (32 feet long)	0	4	0
Side and bilge keelson (32 feet long)	0	4	9
Bulkhead plates, 9 feet × 3 feet 2 inches	0	4	0
,, angle bars	0	1	3
Front of poop bulkhead plates (flush)	0	5	0
Fore and aft deck ties	0	3	0
Diagonal ties	0	3	6
Main hatch fore and afters (main and lower decks)	0	6	0
Poop deck fore and afters	0	5	0
Butt straps	0	0	5
Ditto keel plates	0	0	8
Fore and afters for pall bitt, windlass bitt, and all other scuttle hatches	0	2	6
Framing of forehatch (main and lower deck)	0	4	6
Framing of mainhatch (main and lower deck)	0	6	0
Framing of afterhatch (main and lower deck)	0	4	6
Setting and fitting rudder trunk (complete)	2	0	0

	£	s.	d.
Framing of masts, three plates and two hoops to each (each mast)	1	5	0
Framing for companion, two fore and afters, and two half beams	0	15	0
Framing of skylight, two fore and afters, and four half beams	1	0	0
Making and fitting porthole doors	0	3	6
Cutting and fitting in side lights, 7″ diameter	0	3	6
Ditto, 8″ diameter	0	4	0
Rivets in shell, per 100	0	7	0
Ditto frames	0	6	3
Caulking ship inside and out	40	0	0
Keel rivets, put in by the day, counting 36 rivets as a day's work; all over that number, if sound, to be paid for extra at same rate			
Beam knees	0	1	0
Rudder to be fitted, and plated complete, and put in place, for the sum of	4	0	0
Beam stanchions, making, fitting, and putting in place in ship, each	0	2	0

Screw Steamer of 500 *Tons.*

	s.	d.
Plating garboard strake, per cwt.	3	6
All other strakes, per cwt.	1	8
Setting floors, frames, and reverse bars, each	11	0
Strapping butts, per cwt.	2	6
Packing shell plates, per cwt.	1	6
Main deck and hold beams, per cwt.	2	6
Main deck stringers, per cwt.	2	6
Centre keelson, per cwt.	2	3
Bilge stringer, per cwt.	2	6
Clamp plate, and deck tie-plate, per cwt.	2	0
Engine and boiler seats, per cwt.	2	3
Tunnel, per cwt.	3	6
Coal bunkers, per cwt.	2	6
Tanks, per cwt.	3	0
Boiler hatch and plummer boxes, per cwt.	3	6
Bulkheads, per cwt.	1	9

At the above prices the whole of the work finished ready for riveting. Wages on time, 26s. per week.

Iron Sailing-ship of 800 Tons. Class A a.

	£	s.	d.
Caulking hull	90	0	0
Riveting, ¾" rivets per 100	0	7	6
" ⅞" "	0	9	0
Plating hull, per ton	1	8	4
Inside keelson and bilge stringers, per ton	1	5	0
Bulkheads and centre keelsons, per ton	1	13	4
Setting and finishing frames with reverse bars complete, each	1	7	0
Beams, 'tween decks, and heams with knees attached, each	1	0	0
Deck stringers, per ton	1	5	0
Other iron work, finished and riveted complete, per ton	6	10	0

Screw Steamer of 800 Tons. Class A b.

	s.	d.
Setting frames, floors, and reverse bars, per frame	16	0
Plating garboard strake, per cwt.	3	6
All other strakes, per cwt.	1	4
Bulkheads, per cwt.	1	8
Engine seats and coal-bunkers, per cwt.	2	2
Tunnel, per cwt.	3	6
Boiler hatch and plummer boxes, per cwt.	3	6
Centre keelson, per cwt.	1	8
Main deck and hold heams, per cwt.	2	3
Main deck, hold stringers, and tie-plates, per cwt.	2	3
Bilge stringers, per cwt.	1	8
Strapping shell plates, per cwt.	2	0
Packing, per cwt.	1	4

Average Amount of Wages, on Iron Work, per Ton Weight of Material, including Caulking and Riveting, for Vessels Built on the East Coast.

	£	s.	d.
A a, per Ton	5	2	6
A b, "	4	10	0
A c, "	4	2	6

Iron Decks.

Plates 12 ft. long × 20 ins. wide × $\frac{3}{8}$ ins. thick. Rivets $\frac{9}{16}$ diam., $1\frac{3}{8}''$ long, $2\frac{1}{2}''$ pitch.
Butts quadruple riveted, opposite the hatches, remainder double. Strips fore and aft $4\frac{1}{2}''$ wide.

	s.	d.
Punching and countersinking, each plate	3	9
Riveting, per hundred	4	0
Caulking, per yard	0	4

All edges of plates planed at a machine.

East Coast of England.

Cost of an Iron Paddle Steamer of the following Dimensions:—215 × 25 × 13 = 665 *Tons; Half-Poop Deck 50 feet long, and Topgallant Forecastle.*

	£	s.
Iron material, 227 tons	1965	0
Wages—Framing	563	0
,, Plating	180	10
,, Caulking, &c.	356	0
,, Riveting,	460	0

Timber.

	£	s.
For Joiner-work	1110	0
,, Shipwrights	200	0
Wages for Joiners	529	10
,, Shipwrights	290	0

Painting, Glazing, Carving, &c.

	£	s.
Paints	125	0
Glass	12	0
Wages—Painting	96	0
,, Gilding	18	15
,, Carving	30	0
Iron outfit, 240 cwt.	112	0
Wages on ditto	347	0
Castings, 70 cwt.	34	0
Galvanizing iron-work	2	15
Carried forward	£6431	10

	£	s.
Brought forward	6431	10
One pair patent pumps	25	0
Masts and spars materials	88	0
Wages on ditto	30	10
Hemp rope	91	0
Wire rope	33	0
Rigging wages	32	0
Chain for rigging	31	10
Blocks, sheaves, &c.	35	0
Warps, 15 cwt.	27	0
Sails and awnings	229	10
Chains, 111 cwt.	114	0
Anchors, 58 cwt.	75	0
Windlass (patent)	70	0
Boats (four)	83	0
Patent lowering gear	21	0
Steering wheel	5	10
Binnacles and compasses	30	0
Two double-purchase 2-ton cranes, complete	148	0

Cabinet and Upholstery Work.

	£	s.
Timber	71	0
Upholstery	330	0
Wages	81	10
French polishing	27	10
Stained glass	12	0
Marble slabs	15	0
Mirrors	8	10
Cabin clock	4	0
Carving (inside work)	68	0
Plumber, brass work, &c.	327	0
Side-lights, 55 assorted	56	0
Two patent water-closets	15	0
Cabin stoves	7	0
Cooking-range and utensils	40	0
Lamps (including cabin, signal, and others)	19	10
Hardware	172	0
Outfit stores	60	0
Sundry expenses	60	0
Yard and machinery expenses	500	0
	£9484	10

The above was a handsomely fitted Passenger Steamer.

Cost of the following Outfit for an Iron Sailing-ship of 755 *Tons O. M. built to the* A a *Class at Lloyd's, on the* 600-*ton Scale.*

	£	s.
Metal work	74	0
Cementing inside bottom with Portland Cement	38	10
Making wood masts and spars, and providing blocks and dead-eyes	112	15
Cost of timber for spars, &c.	287	0
Ditto spare spars	42	0
Two iron lower masts and bowsprit, with tops, cheeks, caps, &c., complete	250	0
Wire rope for rigging	153	10
Hemp rope for mizen rigging, hawsers, &c.	377	10
Wages for rigging (bending sails not included)	60	0
Sails (making)	197	0
Sails (canvas)	475	0
Brass and plumber work	70	10
Carved work	28	0
Boats complete	70	0
Chain-cables, small chains, and anchors	364	0
French polishing	12	0
Upholstery work	37	10
Galley range	13	0
Compasses, binnacles, barometer, adjustment, &c.	44	10
Flags and books	12	0
Signal lamps	5	0
Tinners' stores	43	0
Electro-plated goods	24	0
Crockery ware	4	10
Medicine chest	7	10
Steering wheel	5	0
Patent windlass	120	0
Cooperage	21	0
Portable forge	3	10
Galvanizing iron-work	7	0
	£2969	5

Cost of an Iron Screw Coasting-vessel of the following Dimensions:— 160 × 20 × 12"6 = 315 *Tons; Half-Poop and Monkey Forecastle; no Passenger Accommodation.*

	£	s.
Wood account	450	10
Iron ,,	1717	0
Smiths' ,,	155	0
Anchors, &c.	140	0
Boats (two)	34	0
Plumber work	60	0
Upholstery work	10	0
Compasses	22	10
Wire rigging	17	0
Hemp rope, &c.	57	0
Sails, &c.	70	0
Furnishings	231	0
Outfit of blocks, &c.	9	5
Cabinet work	12	0
Winches	23	0
Total workmanship	1544	0
Sundry expenses	75	0
	£4627	5

Cost of an Iron Sailing-ship of the following Dimensions:—150 × 28 × 18 = 555 *Tons; built on the* 400-*ton Scale for Lloyd's* A a *Class; Half-Poop and Topgallant Forecastle.*

	£	s.
Iron for ship, 5093 cwt.	2342	0
,, smiths, 111 cwt.	50	0
Rivets, 304 cwt.	187	0
Carpenters' wood	527	0
Joiners' wood	200	0
Hardware	40	0
Tool account	152	10
Coal ,,	29	15
Plant ,,	26	0
Paint, labour, glass, and glazing	107	10
Cementing labour	10	0
Material	26	15
Iron workers' wages	1200	0
Carried forward	£4898	10

	£	s.
Brought forward	4898	10
Smiths' ,,	75	0
Joiners' ,,	215	0
Sawyers' ,,	25	0
Sundry expenses	126	0
Metal work, including ship's pumps	97	0
Brass and plumber work	86	10
Carved work	26	0
Polishing and varnishing	11	10
Upholstery work	33	0
Galvanizing iron work	6	0
Steering wheel	4	10
Survey fees and expenses	36	0
Screw steering gear	22	10
Cabin stove	5	0
Carpenters' wages	309	10
	£5977	0

Hull complete in cabins and fittings, cost as above.

Outfit.

	£	s.
Iron for main and fore lower masts and bowsprit	85	0
Labour on same, smiths' work not included	67	0
Smiths' iron, 140 cwt.	64	0
,, wages	75	0
Timber for spars	150	0
,, outfit	40	0
Making spars and cost of outfit of blocks, &c.	83	0
Hemp rope	160	0
Sundry rope and yarn for rigging	72	0
Riggers' wages	55	0
Sails and patent for the topsails	523	0
Boats	05	0
Anchors, 86 cwt.	57	0
Cables and hawsers	216	0
Small chain, 47 cwt.	32	0
Medicine chest	7	10
Galley, range, and utensils	12	0
Outfit of flags	15	0
Signal lamps	5	0
Carried forward	£1783	10

	£	s.
Brought forward	1783	10
Compasses and adjustment	34	0
Guns, &c.	18	0
Tinners' stores	30	0
Crockery	12	10
Cooperage	27	0
Fire engines	20	0
Paint outfit	26	0
	£1951	0

CLYDE DISTRICT.

Cost of an Iron Screw Coasting Passenger Steamer of the following Dimensions: — 210 × 26 × 15 = 699 *Tons.*

	£	s.
Shipwrights' work	499	5
Joiners' work	450	0
Iron work	1812	10
Joiners' timber	370	0
Shipwrights' timber	725	0
Keel-bars and stem	70	0
Stern-frame	110	0
Rudder forging	34	0
Angle and bulb iron	690	0
Plate iron	2400	0
Rivets	278	0
Hardware	120	0
Store goods (sundry)	150	0
Smiths' work and material	425	0
Turning and fitting brass stanchions, &c.	79	0
Castings, timber heads, &c.	37	10
,, brass work	19	0
Yard expenses, &c.	281	0
Staging, insurance, ropes, &c.	150	0
Rigging, &c.	96	0
Sails, covers, awnings, &c.	213	10
Blocks, outfit, &c.	31	0
Riggers' wages	50	0
Boats (four)	72	0
Cementing inside (Portland)	37	0
Anchors, chains, &c.	250	0
Carried forward	£9449	15

	£	s.
Brought forward	9449	15
Water tanks (two)	48	0
Signal guns	26	0
Clock for cabin	4	10
Patent log, barometer, telescope, &c.	15	0
Lamps, &c.	17	0
Flags	15	10
Boatswain's stores	6	0
Cabin stores, &c.	50	0
Cooperage	16	0
Galley range and utensils	38	0
Ornamental tiles for galley	9	0
Compasses and adjusting	36	10
Plumbers' work throughout	195	0
Carved work, head and stern	30	0
,, ,, inside	42	0
French polishing	14	0
Upholstery work	90	0
Glazing, stained glass, &c.	20	0
Painting	125	0
Survey expenses	45	0
	£10,292	5

The above vessel was fitted up in a superior style; classed *A b* at Lloyd's. Total quantity of iron in vessel, 364 tons.

Cost of an Iron Screw Coasting-vessel, 190 × 28 × 14 *(Hold)* = 722 *Tons, Full Poop, Forecastle, and House amidships; Accommodation for* 30 *Passengers; Rig, Three Pole Masts; Plainly Fitted and Strongly Built; not to Lloyd's or Underwriters' Rules, but a very suitable Vessel for general purposes.*

IRON WORK.

	Tons.	cwt.	qrs.	£	s.	d.
Frames and floors	38	10	2	301	18	10
Wages on ditto				170	3	8
Beams	11	5	2	86	9	2
Wages on beams				15	14	9
Plates, &c.	118	14	0	1062	1	4
Carried forward	168	10	0	£1636	7	9

58 PRACTICAL IRON SHIPBUILDING.

	Tons. cwt. qrs.	£ s. d.
Brought forward	168 10 0	1636 7 9
Wages on plates, &c.	.. ....	488 5 3
Stem	0 18 1	13 19 6
Wages on stem	.. ....	7 8 6
Stern post	2 2 1	88 9 0
Wages on stern post	.. ....	7 2 10
Bulkheads	7 9 1	69 10 9
Wages on bulkheads	.. ....	27 11 9
Rudder	1 15 1	32 17 1
Wages on rudder	.. ....	37 14 2
Stringers	22 0 3	182 0 7
Wages on stringers	.. ....	69 6 7
Keelsons	4 14 0	35 11 11
Wages on keelsons	.. ....	41 16 9
Engine seat	4 6 3	42 13 6
Wages on engine seat	.. ....	24 2 8
Extras for engine seat	.. ....	2 8 4
Coal bunkers	4 19 3	45 6 1
Wages on coal bunkers	.. ....	43 19 2
Moulding iron	2 5 0	15 8 9
Wages on moulding iron	.. ....	11 2 0
Tanks	1 7 3	17 18 4
Wages on tanks	.. ....	27 0 0
Hatches	6 5 3	57 0 6
Wages on hatches	.. ....	40 15 6
Davits	1 15 2	15 19 7
Wages on davits	.. ....	12 13 6
Anchor davits	0 5 2	2 19 5
Wages on anchor davits	.. ....	1 16 10
Hold stanchions	1 14 0	15 6 6
Wages on hold stanchions	.. ....	4 8 11
Timber heads	1 3 0	10 8 4
Wages on timber heads	.. ....	4 13 6
Hawsepipes	0 16 0	6 11 5
Wages on hawsepipes	.. ....	5 15 10
	232 18 3	£3147 1 1

SUNDRY JOBS.

	Material.	Wages.
	£ s. d.	£ s. d.
Covering pipes	0 12 9	6 10 9
Moulds and patterns	4 15 4	10 11 1
Model	4 8 10	
Carried forward	£9 16 11	£17 1 10

	Material.			Wages.		
	£	s.	d.	£	s.	d.
Brought forward	9	16	11	17	1	10
Shores and keel blocks	0	8	4	25	12	5
Sets	0	19	10			
Sundry jobs				15	0	6
Watchman				11	6	9
Expenses of trial trip	6	2	0	3	17	8
Arranging and sorting iron				19	19	4
Allowances to men				4	11	4
Paint	67	14	10	40	4	3
Mast steps and chocks	4	13	5	3	19	7
Steering gear and grating	13	14	8	23	7	6
Ditto alterations	0	5	7	0	11	9
Cementing	28	12	0	7	11	9
Windows	10	12	1	2	18	11
Pumps and water-closets	3	7	7	6	9	10
Scuppers	0	17	6	0	12	10
Chain stoppers	2	19	0	2	4	3
Launch	13	5	6	45	3	10
Ribands	3	6	8	3	8	8
Towing vessel	3	5	0			
Rigging-blocks, &c.	184	8	9	90	12	1
	£354	9	8	£324	15	1

WOOD WORK.

	Material.			Wages.		
	£	s.	d.	£	s.	d.
Decks	202	11	9	52	18	3
Waterways	40	0	11	20	2	2
Masts and spars	66	17	2	23	11	1
Ceiling, all close, no sparring	157	7	4	47	18	0
Rails and metalling	47	10	9	36	14	3
Bulwarks	17	5	1	31	2	10
Gangways	2	0	8	2	7	7
Stanchions	0	12	6	0	11	2
Catheads	5	8	8	3	9	4
Stern mouldings, &c.	2	16	3	1	5	2
Forecastle	10	19	4	4	6	7
Fenders	3	10	2	1	5	11
Ladders	6	7	10	7	11	10
Bucket racks	0	7	0	0	10	7
Carried forward	£563	15	5	£233	14	9

	Material.	Wages.
	£ s. d.	£ s. d.
Brought forward	563 15 5	233 14 9
Lamp stands	0 3 0	0 16 10
Flag-staff	0 2 6	0 8 0
Carving and wood	22 8 1	5 0 0
Seats for top of poop	1 2 0	1 11 6
Hatches	63 17 7	25 9 6
Mooring bits and chocks	1 5 3	0 5 4
	£652 13 10	£267 5 11

OUTFIT.

	Material.	Wages.
	£ s. d.	£ s. d.
Main cabin (1st class)	146 10 7	98 11 10
After cabin (2nd class)	89 9 0	46 9 10
Skylights	14 7 1	9 10 4
Meat safe	1 0 7	1 2 9
Patent capstan	75 0 0	
Small warping capstan	7 10 0	
Capstan fixings	11 7 6	6 8 6
Mahogany tables for cabins	5 9 0	2 2 2
Settees	2 17 5	2 4 11
Sideboard	7 10 9	5 17 3
Wash-stands	0 19 0	0 12 0
Sundries	19 0 7	0 12 7
Derricks for cargo	2 14 1	2 4 1
Crab winch	11 0 0	0 7 8
Grindstone and trough	0 9 8	0 6 2
Cooper work	7 7 7	0 18 9
Binnacles	2 8 9	0 16 3
Binnacle bell	1 12 0	
Ship's bell and frame	4 18 10	0 4 4
Anchors, 63 cwt. 2 qrs.	67 10 6	0 4 10
Cables, 189 cwt.	108 14 0	
Side lamps, &c.	7 6 0	
Painting and gilding	101 1 6	
Glazing	18 0 0	
Hawsers	30 5 6	
Upholstery	44 0 0	
Plumber work	88 10 0	
Nautical instruments	21 14 3	
Carried forward	£898 14 2	£178 14 3

PRACTICAL IRON SHIPBUILDING. 61

	Material.	Wages.
	£ s. d.	£ s. d.
Brought forward	898 14 2	178 14 3
Sails, covers, &c.	120 2 0	
Steering lamp	3 6 0	
Flags	7 12 0	
Hen coops	1 14 6	1 13 7
Galley, with range and utensils	44 8 8	3 2 6
Accommodation ladders	5 16 7	10 15 7
Boats (four)	39 19 4	38 18 2
Iron railing, 22 cwt.	17 6 0	22 17 8
Awning stanchions	8 17 5	2 5 6
	£1147 16 8	£258 7 3

EPITOME.

	£ s. d.
Iron-work, material	2104 11 9
Iron-work, wages	1042 9 4
Sundry jobs, material	354 9 8
Sundry jobs, wages	324 15 1
Wood-work, material	652 13 10
Wood-work, wages	267 5 11
Outfit, material	1153 16 8
Outfit, wages	258 7 3
	£6158 9 6

To the above costs must be added a sufficient percentage to cover working expenses, such as rent, wear of machinery, coals, foremen's wages, &c. Such percentage may in most cases can be put down at 10 per cent.

Decimal Multipliers for giving the Weights in Cwts. or Tons of any number of Square Feet of Wrought-iron Plate.

Thickness.	Multiplier for Cwts.	Multiplier for Tons.
$1''$	·3571	·01785
$\frac{7}{8}''$	·31248	·015624
$\frac{3}{4}''$	·26784	·013392
$\frac{5}{8}''$	·22320	·011160
$\frac{9}{16}''$	·20088	·010044
$\frac{1}{2}''$	·17856	·008924
$\frac{7}{16}''$	·15624	·007812
$\frac{3}{8}''$	·13392	·006696
$\frac{5}{16}''$	·11160	·005580
$\frac{1}{4}''$	·08928	·004464
$\frac{3}{16}''$	·06696	·003348
$\frac{1}{8}''$	·04464	·002232
$\frac{1}{16}''$	·002232	·001116

Note.—The number of square feet of plating, multiplied by the multiplier proper to the thickness, will give weight as required in cwts. or tons, according to the multiplier used.

The square foot of inch-plate is supposed to equal 40 lbs. Bad iron weighs a little less, and extra quality a little over.

To Steam Packet Companies, Shipowners, &c.

T. SMITH will be glad to furnish Designs, Estimates of Cost, Specifications, and Models, for every description of Naval Architecture, and to inspect the Building of Vessels, or value the same.

The accompanying are a few of the Vessels *designed and built under his superintendence* :—

"Nelly," *Paddle Yacht;* "Norah Creina," *Screw Yacht;* "Tayr Neil," *Paddle Yacht;* "Tanghta," *Paddle Yacht;* "Tycoon," *Armed Screw Yacht;* "Colleen Bawn," *Drogheda Steam Packet Co.;* "Chile," "Quito," "Payta," "Pacifico," &c., *Pacific Steam Navigation Co.;* "Emerald Isle," "Danton," "Kenilworth," "Surprise," "Erin's Pride," &c., *Sailing Vessels;* "Cologne," and "Taurus," *General Steam Navigation Co.;* "Macgregor Laird," and "Calabar," *African Mail Co.;* "Ipojuca," and "Pirapama," *Pernambuco Steamship Co.;* "Falcon," "Flamingo," "Evelyn," and "Raven," *Swift Despatch Paddle Packets.*

SEAFORT AVENUE, SANDYMOUNT,
DUBLIN, 1869.

LONDON:
PRINTED BY WILLIAM CLOWES AND SONS, STAMFORD STREET,
AND CHARING CROSS.

www.ingramcontent.com/pod-product-compliance
Lightning Source LLC
Chambersburg PA
CBHW030119010526
44116CB00005B/317